IN THE SHADOW OF DEATH

First published by Dog Ear Publishing
4010 W. 86th Street, Ste H
Indianapolis, IN 46268
www.dogearpublishing.net

ISBN: 978-1-4575-1443-2

This book is printed on acid-free paper.

Printed in the United States of America

To the memories of my little brother Swen,
Uncle Milton and all the family members
that died during the course of the Civil War.

To all the women and children of Liberia
and other war torn countries around the world
who lost their lives to war.

IN THE SHADOW OF DEATH

Growing up during the Liberian Civil War

HANS GIPLAYE

CHAPTER

One

SAMUEL DOE LED A COUP D'ÉTAT that overthrew the elected government of Liberia in 1980, the very year I was born in the town of Yekepa in Nimba county in the north central part of the country. Yekepa was a beautiful city then. Walking around with different problems in life, Liberians from different tribes and cultural back grounds lived there.

My neighborhood was a mysterious and exciting place to be. In the distance, beyond the swamp in front of my house was a badly maintained cocoa farm. The owner did not clear the brush regularly. But that was okay by me, because it was a perfect hiding place for my friends and me during our games of hide and seeks. Visiting my friends down the street, I would walk and run down a narrow path. Flowers bloomed in the grass along the edges. At the end of this narrow path was a muddy, dirty brown walking trail running into the green forest at the back of the city. It went on forever.

I was the first person to wake up every morning when I heard my father moving around the house getting ready for his work as an assistant engineer at the Swedish/German mining company, LIMCO. As he hurried to work, I stood in the door and waved him off as he shifted the two-door

Volkswagen Beetle into gear and took off. I used to laugh at the car because I thought it was stupid to have the engine at the back where the trunk was supposed to be while other cars had their engines in the front. Then, our nanny Rose helped me and my five siblings get ready for school. My mother was a small business woman who ran her bakery business from home. When Rose escorted us to the school bus stop, the air was crisp and cool smelling with sweet smell of wild flowers.

After school before doing our home work, my friends and I would go swimming at the little river on the edge of town. It felt so good. The warm temperature of the water against the cooler air created a drifting airy atmosphere that whispered over the river. We air dried ourselves on the rocks on the river banks as the warm breezes from the south graced our skin. Hours later, my friends and I headed our separate ways home as the darkness enveloped the sky setting the perfect stage for the twinkling stars in the clear skies. If I was late coming home, there was someone who cared, and who would come looking for me. A warm, well prepared dinner awaited me at home. These surely were the good old days.

On most Friday evenings, my dad would take me with him on one of his night shifts working on the rail road, changing track up in the mountains between Liberia and the country of Guinea. I would ride in the front seat with my dad poking my head out the passenger side window enjoying the cool breeze as the pickup truck struggled to reach the peak of the windy mountain. I could see the bright green rainforest stretched as far as my eyes could see as my brain try to comprehend. Minutes later, the car would roll down the hill in free gear into the thick jungle canopy as the sunlight from the beautiful sunset filtered through to grace the forest floor below.

My parents told me stories of the atrocities committed by President Samuel K. Doe. Doe and his followers killed President William Tolbert and later executed most of his cabinet members. President Doe established a military regime called the People's Redemption Council and enjoyed early support from a large number of indigenous Liberian tribes who had been excluded from power since the founding of the country in 1847 by freed American slaves. Doe, himself, was from the Krahn tribe and gave most of his government was Krahn. Any hope that Doe would change the way Liberia was run was fading.

And I remember the attempted coup of 1985. Thomas Quiwonkpa, the former Commanding General of the Armed Forces of Liberia, who Doe had demoted and forced to flee the country, came back and attempted to overthrow Doe's regime from neighboring Sierra Leone in November of that year.

It was a beautiful morning when Thomas Quiwonkpa attempted his coup which turned into a brutal blood bath. For hours, we were locked indoors, hiding under the beds, in the closets, and in bath tubs; some adults ran into the bush for their dear lives. When it was all over and the curfew was lifted, I came out with Eric, my oldest brother, to check into our neighbor's compound. I saw dead bodies on our neighbor's lawn and front steps. The police later came and took the bodies to the local police station for families to come and claim their dead.

The Gio and Mano ethnic groups, who supported the coup, sang and danced on the streets. We watched them on local television, the men beating drums while the women waved their clothes and woven handkerchiefs in the air. This celebration did not last long. By noon that very day, the Liberian national anthem played on the radio station. After the emergency warning sounded, everyone gathered around their radios and TVs. About sixty seconds later President Samuel K Doe came on. "The coup nearly succeeded, I, Doe, the president, am safe and Quiwonkpa was captured."

President Doe immediately came down to dealing with the perpetrators of the coup, which would later be called "The November business." He announced that all Quiwonkpa supporters be arrested. This announcement unleashed horrific violence on the streets of Liberia. In Nimba County, government soldiers went door to door killing hundreds of Quiwonkpa's supporters, mostly Gio and Mona tribe members. I personally witnessed the bloody beating of some of our neighbors because they were from the Gio and Mano tribes. My family was from the Grabo tribe so we were safe for the moment, but later the fact my father was close friends with our neighbors who were Gio and Mano made us a target.

The police director (police chief) at the time, Mr. Charles Julu, was a personal friend to my father. But he was unable to protect my dad. Because of his work at the mining company, my dad's friends were mostly Gio and Mano. As a result, we became a target of the violence too. In 1986, my dad had to escape to the United States, leaving me and my five siblings, Eric, Catherine, Rita, Matthew, and Lewis in the care of my mother. Eric was the oldest and when our father left, he was supposed to provide guidance and stability when Uncle Milton was not around. But he was just a ten year old boy trying to be a father figure. Later, during the war, he became a child soldier as part of his role "to protect the family." This led to his use of drugs and alcohol to escape the harsh realities of the world.

Catherine was second, and she was about nine years old with dark hair and dark eyes and a smile that could brighten any room. She had to take on the role of mother when our mother was not around. Naturally, this made it more difficult for her to make friends her age. But it did inspire me and the rest of my siblings to strive to be the best that we could be.

Third in line, I was six years old and Rita was five. Following Rita was Matthew, who was four years old, and

Lewis, the youngest, was two. Our mother was pregnant with a child in 1986 before my father escaped to the United States. She delivered a baby boy named Swen before getting a visa two years later to join my father. She had to leave Swen behind along with the rest of us because she could not get a visa for us. We went to live with relatives in the village.

The actions taken during and after the attempted coup established an unprecedented new level of brutality in Liberia and yielded enduring hatred for President Doe, particularly among the Gio and Mano tribes. Charles Taylor exploited this hatred five years later to start a civil war that claimed the lives of more than 250,000 Liberians and displaced hundreds of thousands more as refugees around the world. Thousands of civilians were massacred through the entire country and hundreds of thousands fled their homes. My family and I became part of this mass exodus, travelling from one village to the next.

A child of former slaves who founded Liberia, Charles Taylor worked for Doe's government as a General Services Agency (GSA) director. GSA was responsible for government spending and purchases overseas. But Taylor was fired from Doe's government after being accused of embezzlement of more than $900,000 that was supposed to be used to purchase machine parts. He was arrested in the United States on an extradition warrant and jailed in a Massachusetts minimum security prison. From there, he fought extradition on the ground that he would face assassination in Liberia.

In September, 1985, Taylor apparently escaped from the prison, along with four other inmates. They sawed through a window bar and climbed a fence. All four of Taylor's fellow escapees were eventually rounded up, but Charles Taylor made his way back to Africa.

In Ivory Coast, he assembled a group of rebels (mostly ethnic Gios and Manos who felt persecuted by the Doe government) that later became known as the National Patriotic Front of Liberia (NPFL). They invaded Nimba County on December 24, 1989.

The Liberian Army retaliated against the whole population of the region, attacking unarmed civilians and burning villages. Many left as refugees for Guinea and Ivory Coast, but opposition to Doe was inflamed.

Led by Charles Taylor, the NPFL was a small group of Libyan-trained rebels that recruited child soldiers and angry, unemployed men and women. Its attack on the Nimba County village of Butuo was fearless. Butuo was a prosperous cocoa-growing border town on the Liberia/Ivory Coast border. The raid, mounted by a small group of men, managed to capture some weapons, before the raiders withdrew to the jungle. The NPFL initially encountered plenty of support within Nimba County, which had endured the majority of Samuel Doe's wrath after the 1985 attempted coup.

Soon after the first attack, Doe responded by sending Armed Forces of Liberia (AFL) battalions, including the 1st Infantry Battalion, to Nimba in December 1989-January 1990, under the command of Colonel Hezekiah Bowen. The AFL acted in a brutal and scorched-earth fashion which quickly alienated the local people.

By May 1990, the AFL had been forced back to Gbarnga in neighboring Bong County. They lost Gbarnga after a NPFL assault on May 28, 1990. By June, Taylor's forces were laying siege to the capital, Monrovia.

In July 1990, Prince Yormie Johnson split from Taylor and formed the Independent National Patriotic Front (INPFL). It consisted mostly of Gio tribesmen as he was from the Gio tribe. This split led to more civilian deaths and complicated the entire war situation. Now we had to deal with two rebel groups and government troops that did little, if anything, to protect the Liberian people. The INPFL and NPFL continued laying siege to Monrovia, which the AFL defended. Prince Johnson soon took control of parts of Monrovia prompting evacuation of foreign nationals and diplomats by the U.S. Navy in August 1990.

The sixteen-member Economic Community of West African States (ECOWAS) agreed to deploy a joint military intervention force with the Economic Community Monitoring Group (ECOMOG), and place it under Nigerian leadership. The mission later included troops from non-ECOWAS countries, including Uganda and Tanzania. ECOMOG's objectives were to impose a cease-fire, help Liberians establish an interim government until elections could be held, stop the killing of innocent civilians, and ensure the safe evacuation of foreign nationals. ECOMOG also sought to prevent the conflict from spreading into neighboring states, which share a complex history of state, economic, and ethno-social relations with Liberia.

This brief history told above was the period of my childhood.

CHAPTER

Two

LIBERIA HAS ALWAYS BEEN A poor country, although very blessed with natural resources. Corrupt leaders had always mismanaged the country's resources by taking them all for themselves. By 1990, one in five Liberians had access to safe drinking water. In the countryside where most of the pre-war population resided, only six percent had clean water. Liberia had a population of less than two million at the time of the war.

Barely one in five adults could read or write, and only one in five school-age kids finished elementary school due to the affordability of school fees. Mothers were torn between putting food on the table and paying school fees or medical expenses mostly especially for killer diseases like malaria. The infant mortality at the time was ten times the western world average. Life expectancy was about fifty years old. Believe it or not, those were the good old days or as we Liberians will say "normal days" of Liberia. The worst was yet to come.

A little boy of nine years, I still remember the day very clearly. It was a cold, tropical morning typical of the West African dry season, before the sun rose above the horizon. Nimba County was mountainous so it was also foggy that morning. The crowing of the rooster woke us from our early morning sleep. This was the only alarm clock we knew. I found it a peaceful and bright morning, especially after a long night made restless by the itching of mosquito bites.

Like all African kids, I had to do chores before walking at least three miles to school. My job was to fetch water from the nearby well for my uncle's wife to cook that morning. I walked downhill on this narrow muddy path. As I turned a corner, a group of friends came running from the other direction. We all raced down the unpaved red dusty road sheltered by the tree canopy as birds, toads and crickets sang from a distance. The well was in a field of green grass.

As we headed back home with buckets full of fresh water, we heard a sound that was similar to that of the fireworks that would be used for the Christmas holidays coming up. As we came closer to our homes, the sound became louder and more powerful. We saw men with AK-47 assault rifles. They were dressed in black baggy jeans with deep red T-shirts and red bands around their heads. We all dashed our buckets of water and ran. This was the last time I ever saw most of my friends from the well. According to my uncle, "the rebels had attacked the army barracks, minutes ago." His voice trembled as he said it and his hands were shaking. The sudden outburst of gunfire had caused people to run for their lives in different directions. My friends' parents came running from their workplaces, only to stand in front of the empty houses with no idea of where their families had run to. Mothers wept as they ran toward schools, rivers banks, and to the hill tops where we kids went sliding every day, to look for their children. Children ran home to look for parents. As the gunfire intensified, people became even more frightened and losing hope of looking for their loved ones ran out of town into nearby waste land, swamps and forest to hide.

Some military families made it out of the barracks, some I knew as friends because I used to play soccer with them, but they couldn't tell us the whereabouts of their family members. My friend Yansay's dad was a military officer. Yansay had been peeking through a tiny closet hole when he saw a young fellow that he knew gun down his father in his bedroom. But his mother had left for the market that early morning, so her life was spared. The survivors from the military barrack knew nothing because the attack was too sudden, too chaotic. Frantically, everyone had fled in different locations in total confusion. In fact, as we ran in different directions we were fired upon and some did not make it out alive.

All I remember was Uncle Milton holding Lewis, my little brother who was about five years old at the time, and telling me, Catherine and Rita my little sister to run fast to the cocoa bush. Eric was missing in action because his school was a distance away from our house. It was not safe to try to find him in the middle of the chaos, but he later caught up with us.

The family started running with other families from the neighborhood. There was screaming and shouting everywhere. People crawled and fell to their knees as the gunshots got progressively louder. My breathing was getting heavier and faster, gunshots and explosions were sounding closer and debris from explosions were landing closer and closer around me and the others as we took cover in the cocoa bush.

For more than three hours, we stayed at the cocoa farm in hiding anxiously waiting and expecting either to see our families or to talk to someone who had seen them. But there was no news. After a while, we didn't know any of the people who came running down into the cocoa farm. They were bleeding from their heads, ears, and everywhere. This day seemed very terrifying; I thought this was the end of the world.

But it wasn't; nature stayed its course. Birds sang from treetops, as crickets and toads chirped and croaked from swampland a few feet from us. The sun sailed down through the white clouds as night fell, while the trees swayed wildly. It was a windy evening.

I couldn't believe that the war had actually started, after months of hearing that the rebels were in the forest on the Guinea, Ivory Coast and Liberia border. This seemed impossible. I thought I was dreaming in one of those terrible long nights of sleep, just waiting for one of my siblings to slap me out of it as usual. But this was real, live action and happening.

Three

WHEN I LEFT HOME THAT morning to fetch water, there was no indication that rebels were anywhere near. But something strange was happening that preceded the rebel attack. A couple of days before the rebels attacked, there were many crazy mad men roaming the streets. Nobody cared to ask them where they came from; but instead, we made fun of them as kids will do. We were just kids playing around in the neighborhood laughing at strange people. But when the rebels attacked, these crazy mad men were the majors and captain" leading the rebels through the neighborhoods. We came to find out these guys were not crazy at all, but on a spying mission the entire time. I said to my Uncle Milton, Eric, Lewis, Catherine and Rita, "I remember some of these guys from yesterday and the day before. They were the crazy fellows we made fun of at the river banks and market place yesterday and the day before."

My uncle and Catherine said, "Shut up before you have us all killed." Even though Catherine was about eleven years old, but she was the only mother figure in our lives at this point. To me she was very inspiring and caring as an older sister. Before the war, she had been a very intelligent and brilliant student in her class, and most guys did not like that. Being a girl in African schools was not cool at the time and it was even worse to be smartest in the class. My sister Catherine made the boys look inferior and they hated her for that. When Uncle Milton was not around, Catherine made the decisions and this was very special. She was very concerned that we could be murdered if I kept running my mouth which is why she told me to keep quiet.

Hours later after the gunfire ceased a little, we made our way back home to find most families in disarray and panicked in our neighborhood. As a nine year old, the first thing that ran through my imaginative mind was, "Yea, no school day today!" But what I didn't know was this was just the beginning of the seven years of no school at all. I also did know I was about to witness the wrath, cruelty and barbarity of my own countrymen murdering their own brothers and sisters because of their tribal backgrounds, political affiliations or social-economic status. The killings began between the government forces and the rebels, but quickly moved into the general population.

Those days were no ordinary ones; bloodshed was everywhere. The lovely and lively nature of our cities, towns, and villages had suddenly disappeared and become a den of beasts and monsters, many of them people we knew, people we played with, went to school with, and looked up to as role models and big brothers. Due to the turbulence and chaos created by our brothers, my days and nights went very fast. On most days, time flew because of the anxiety of death that fills the atmosphere, but on some days, time became stagnant, grim and empty as we hid behind closed doors worried about when a gunman would come bursting through the doors, walls or windows to slaughter us all.

As the week went on, young boys began to join the rebels. Most of them were given machetes, clubs or sticks with sharp edges. From what I witnessed, most killings were done with machetes and sharp sticks in order to save bullets for the real soldiers in battle, since bullets were expensive. Over the next few days, the rebels captured the northern town Yekepa, near the Guinean border, and all military posts. The violence spread as the killers went door to door in Yekepa, slaughtering men, women and children. The city was on lockdown as checkpoints and road blocks were established. The government troops were ether murdered or had withdrawn to the nearest town called Sanniquellie. Nowhere was now safe. Neighbors could turn you in to the rebels or vilify you to the Doe government.

Four

IT WAS A SATURDAY MORNING, the skyline was light blue, but the smell of death, sadness and panic filled the air. My uncle took me to go and look for food in looted stores. Many had gotten killed searching for food in vandalized stores, but I was always his right hand man. He took me where ever he went because even though I was only nine, I was the next oldest male and would have to provide for the family if he was killed. On our way back, we saw a blaze of fire coming from Area B where our house was located. Area B was a company quota, an area of free housing units provided to all LIMCO employees. The rebels attacked had attacked this area with a Russian Powerful Gun (RPG), because they believed some of the government officials lived there.

During the assault, my family house was hit by a rocket. While my uncle and I were gone in search for food, seven of our family members died on the spot including my little brother Swen, three years old at the time; my uncle's pregnant wife, Theresa; and his two sons. My aunt Esther and her husband Jayswen were also dead on the scene. My grandma was hurt in the leg and my little brother, Matthew, who was four years old at the time, had a split jaw. Aunty

Emma, Catherine, Rita, Eric and Lewis had minor injuries. We made it out of the area as fast as we could so that we would not be spotted by rebels and be tortured and killed. For the others, the bombed house was their place of burial.

The area was still under attack, there was no time to mourn or cry for the dead. My tears trickled down my face and my mouth quavered. Uncle Milton's legs and feet trembled. But we took a wheelbarrow, put grandma, Lewis and Matthew in it, and ran out of the compound in fear. Starting to throw up because of the fresh blood dripping from the grandma's leg, I helped my little brother Matthew. He was bleeding from his jaw and gut.

As we escaped between narrow corridors of houses and made it to the main road, we saw a small group of people running towards the Yekepa Assembly of God church compound down the road. Some were desperately running for their lives and did not even know that they were badly wounded with some of their body parts hanging of their bodies. Some folks managed to leave their homes with cloth bundles of what they needed to survive. We all went screaming in the church compound for refuge. I held back my sorrows to mourn my dead brother and other family members another day. Two days, Emma who was a nurse by profession try to applied pressure dressings on grandma and Matthew wounds but it did not work. So she decided to take them to the local hospital to seek better medical attention, and that was the last time we ever saw Emma, Matthew and grandma Nancy.

I saw men and women wounded with peel off skin hanging off of arms and legs. Fresh blood mixed with dirt clotted on their bodies. I saw a man carrying his wounded son as blood dropped from his fingers and rolled down his elbows. This little boy's body had bullet holes in the chest and neck. His brave and terrified dad carried his injured and weak body hoping to save his life. So many wounded in that church compound, but there was no nurse or doctor around to help. I heard the dad with the little boy call him Saydee as he cried. Minutes later, Saydee died from his injuries and severe blood loss. His innocent lifeless body was buried at the back of the church with others who died that morning.

More people had been wounded by stray bullets during the attack as we escaped the rebels that morning; many later died from the injuries in the church compound. The death in the church compound was so high; the area underneath the breadnut trees was turned into a cemetery.

My friend Seneh died in the church compound from infection of his wounds and dehydration from diarrhea. He and I were so close that I considered him family. He was one of the oldest of the neighborhood kids that I hung out with, playing soccer every day. His parents were killed when they tried to escape, and he was wounded but was able to make it into the compound covered with blood.

I did not feel much pain when he passed, but it hit me really hard when he was being lowered into the hole at the back of the church. Standing from a distance, I saw four men using the rope to lower his body with no coffin, and then the pastor said a little prayer than the men started covering him with the red African earth as if the earth itself was soaked with blood. I felt my heart drop into my chest; I felt faint and lightheaded and I became short of breath. After that I started to sob and my uncle came and took me in the church to sit with Mama Yaah and the rest of the family.

Later on, I peeked through the window and I saw the men who had lowered Seneh's body placing rocks around the grave to hold the mounds of earth in place. That very day, it rained hard as if God was mad about the death of the innocent souls whose beautiful lives were prematurely shortened.

Soon after that, a woman placed her dead baby at the altar. Her body was covered with blood from holding her injured child through the night hoping for a miracle by day break. "God whyyy?" Her mourning cry was so powerful, it echoed through the entire compound. This cry from a grieving mother expressed the pain and sorrow of other grieving mothers later in the war then, today and the future as long Africa continues to be plagued with conflicts and wars.

Five

I THOUGHT WE WERE SAFE living in that church compound. For weeks, we lived there, waiting for the trouble to
be over outside. In the morning, Pastor Moses would
preach and pray for everyone. I listened to him talk about
the end times from the book of Matthew in the Bible. I
remembered heard him say all the time during his preaching, "To be happy, one must believe in the one and only
higher power which is God by coming to Jesus Christ, the
son of God." After his preaching, many went to the altar,
including me. I was among the group every morning that
went for altar calls. It did not matter if I had gone forward
the day before, because I just wanted to be saved by God
from those crazy rebels.

During the day, the courageous ones among us, including my uncle and me ventured out into the surrounding
fields to bring back food. In fact, as a boy growing up in that
bush, I knew the location of more cassava, potatoes and
rice farms in the area than my uncle and other adults. At
night, there was a feeling of sadness everywhere, wheezing
sounds from crying, as able men consoled the women.

Embracing the darkness, we slept inside or outside,
according to who was weak and strong. Over fifty percent of

us in that compound were wounded, some had bloody patches to the head or an eye, while some had minor to deep wounds to their legs and arms wrapped with torn cloth or T-Shirts. Pastor Moses prayed, as we all hoped for better news the next day.

Every morning, grown up men sat around in panic and listened to BBC News on one satellite radio; the stories of the killings outside sounded so exaggerated they were hard to believe. Pastor Moses and other elders knew more because they had a small black and white TV in the tiny back office/bedroom, and were watching everything on TV. But they did not tell us, because they did not want us to be more terrified and panic. Unlike the movie "Hotel Rwanda", most of the white missionaries left the country before the rebel attack, because they knew what was about to happen but did not warn anyone because their consulate offices told them not to, just to avoid panic and make their escape easy. Most foreign nationals were already evacuated to nearby countries before the rebels attacked and captured them.

One morning, the rebels started making advances toward the Church compound after some rumors spread that there were escaped Krahn tribe people and government troops hiding out there. Some cars came inside the fence with armed men at the back of a Toyota pickup. Pastor Moses went to confront the leader and plead for our life, but they shot him down. Shocked, I and everyone else ran into the church building. The commanders ordered his boys to shoot at the door. We started piling up the chairs and anything we could find just to prevent that door from opening.

But our resistance did not have much force behind it. Boom! A grenade exploded at the front door. I was positioned at the back with other kids and saw blood splashes on the walls and body parts fly in all directions. My heart pounded faster and my breathing became heavy as I raced down to the back door with other kids to find our way over the fence. We scattered into the swampy land at the back of the church compound. I ran so furiously, I don't know how I ended up to my hiding position. All I can remember is lying in a pile of mud with dead bodies all around me. I heard chattering sounds in all directions as other kids dove for cover.

Minutes later, dead silence. I dared not make any noise. I knew the reputation of this bush to be full of snakes and other dangerous plants and bugs. I had this sinking feeling that I would not make it out of this place. I was petrified and scared, especially when I saw the dead bodies and empty slingshots in the swamp; I knew this was a killing valley.

At this moment, I did not of course have any idea where Uncle Milton and my brother Eric, Lewis, sister Rita and, Catherine. For the next few days, I was prepared to spend my days in the mud, covered from head to toe, under the tyranny of the mosquitoes, bugs and snakes. But hours later, the able men, including my uncle, had the courage to surface and start gathering us into groups. Right after they had finished shooting at us in the swamp, they had gotten into in their cars and taken off, but we dared not return to that church compound again that day.

In the morning, we could not even give ourselves a moment to dry out in the rising sun. The adults took us children, soaked through with dirty water and mud, in little groups under the cover of the wild sugar cane bushes. They told us to take cover and be very quiet because the bad hide and seek was about to happen, meaning not to put more than a head out of the water and not to cry. We drank the muddy water draining from the swamp, even if it was sometimes tinged with blood and smells of decaying bodies. We would glimpse one another through the surrounding foliage. I asked myself, why God had forsaken us here, in the midst of snakes, which fortunately did not bite anyone. Thank God for that.

After freezing, cold nights and hot, humid days of living in the swamp with corpses everywhere; badly suffering from mosquito bites and listening to toe frogs and crickets sing all night, fear and panic plagued my mind. Some people gave up and left the swamps to go to the town hall, hoping for some protection from the local authorities because their kids were getting weaker. But they found out the hard way that rebels had already taken over all government buildings, murdered all government officials that did not escape before the rebels got there, and dragged their bodies across town behind Toyota pickups and other looted vehicles. One thing everyone who escaped into the bush had figured out was how to stay alive from then on. If you stayed in town, you would be killed.

During those days of hiding in the swamp, all kids went down a muddy path at the base of the slop very early in the morning to drink from the dirty water and do head count by elders in the group. After that, the little ones hid first, the grown-ups acted as look-outs and talked about the disaster that had befallen us. They were the last to hide. We lived mostly on raw cassava and raw plantain.

All day long there was the killing. In the beginning, the rebels would come and just shoot everywhere in the swamp, singing and yelling out, "YOU rat come out." The most petrified and panicky ones got up and were massacred standing. The sound of flying bullets passed my head like a race car going by thousand miles an hour. The fizzing sound of a human being hit by the bullets near and far from me was very distinct from any other sound. Then came heavy breathing, panting, and legs jerking in the mud. Fingers twitched slowly before they took their last breath with eyes still wide open. The smell, sounds and feeling of death lingered in the swamp.

The killers came in the morning, worked in the swamps through the day, than about half past noon, as the sun set in the middle of the sky, they left. Sometimes, if it rained too much, they came later in the morning and stayed until sunset. They came in small groups, announcing their arrival with songs and whistles. They beat drums and shot their weapons in the sky. They sounded very excited to be going killing for an entire day.

Each morning, they would take a new path, and the next day another path using their machetes to make new paths like a crop circle. When we heard the first whistles or song, we disappeared in the opposite direction and took cover. During the evenings, they cheated. They came from all sides springing traps and ambushes, spraying bullets in the swamp and that day was a very disheartening one because we knew that evening there would be more than the usual number of dead. If you did not see your loved one during head count at the base of the slop the next morning, they had over slept, they were gone for good. Mothers would tightly hold their stomachs and sob quietly because the little boy or girl did not wake up.

In the afternoon, they (the killers) would not sing anymore because they were tired, but chattered away as they returned to their homes. They fortified themselves with drink and by eating the cows that they had slaughtered at the same time as the Krahn and anyone who did not join their quest for blood and revenge. These were truly very calm and accomplished killings. Even more terrifying, these were boys that we all grew up with. But they were different in the doing: red eyes, wag on the head, warrior songs as they called them.

When they spotted a small group of runaways trying to escape by creeping through the mud, they called us rats. Before the killings, some rebel usually referred to us as Jews. But during the killings, it was more suitable to call their victims Krahn rats, because of their attitude, or zeros, or dogs, because in our country most people don't like dogs. In any case we were less-than-nothings.

23

"Nevertheless, we have to find our way out," said my uncle, "This is a dumping ground for the rebels. That is why we have corpses everywhere. We must leave here now, because the rebels will find us when they come to dump their next bodies."

At this point, all my hope had dried up standing in this mass grave, the dragon flies beating on my forehead as vultures circled overhead in the sky looking for their daily meals on the corpses. Frightened, but as an optimist, I believed that if I still had breath in my lungs, there was still hope and opportunity in every calamity. My intuition told me that I ran with thousands of people out of that church compound; I was still alive for a purpose.

We stumbled on corpses upon corpses as we wiggled our way through the swamp. Stepping on skulls and bodies of babies, women and men; I remember seeing an old woman. She was already lying almost dead on the ground, her body buried in the mud except her bloody head and arms sticking out slowly moving. My uncle said there was no need to try saving her because she was already dead. So I covered my face and turned the other way as I jumped over her. Newly dumped bodies still had fresh blood oozing out of the bullet holes and some still flapping their limbs and moving their mouths like a fish taken out of the water gasping for oxygen to live.

Six

THE NEXT DAY AS WE scrambled to escape Yekepa, eighteen-year-old Sawinaah came running to my uncle's friend's house. We were staying with the friend because my Uncle Milton thought it was a safe place. Sawinaah, an extended family member, told us how the rebels cut down some folks alive and on their feet in the church compound like the logging company cutting down a forest. "It was the day of the massacre at the church," he said, "a very evil day."

When we heard that story, my uncle could not believe it. My uncle thought he was in one of the last groups of elders to make it out alive with my little brother Lewis in his arm as he carried Rita by one hand through the fence.

"The killers have left town," said Sawinaah. "We can go and find out ourselves at the church. People are going there to find their love ones."

During the uproar in the church, I thought we all had made it out. When the grenade had exploded on the opposite side of the church door, we had all run for the back door. But my uncle explained to me that there were strong men and boys who held down the door while we, the women and children, escaped.

When my uncle said this, my legs went numb and shaky the room started to close in on me as, and my body temperature switched between hot and cold at the same time because friends and extended family members had been with us in the church compound. When we did not find them in the swamp days later, we hoped they had run the other way. With this news coming from Sawinaah, I was shocked and terrified.

Sawinaah, Uncle Milton and I carefully ran about a mile down the street to check out the news he brought to us. The compound was deadly silent when we entered; there was no movement except for the flies flying out of the doors and windows. My uncle and the other survivors from the swamp entered the church while Sawinaah kept me on the front porch because I was too little to see such a brutal scene. Minutes went by, and I heard grunting, so I ran from Sawinaah around the back to see what was happening by peeking through concrete block window. In the sun light filtering through the glass windows, the dead were visible between the pews. Corpses crumbled beneath the pews, and more dead were in the aisles on the way to the foot of the altar. We were the only moving people at that moment in that church. I said to myself, if God could not save these people after all the long mornings, days and night of prayers, who can he save.

On the other hand, I added, "I am lucky to be standing here alive," But why were our lives spared?

There was no safe haven anymore. When we came into the compound, we believed it was God's House and we would be protected, but without knowing it, we were waiting for death in the comfort of our faith in a church. We had prayed for help and God's protection day after day, but some believed God had turned his back on us that afternoon. For the most part, I wanted to be part of the dead in the church. I believed there was nowhere better to be killed than in a church.

It appeared as if the killers had verified the identity of each person, inspected their faces, so as to finish off everyone conscientiously. With no fear that the Almighty God was watching them, they dragged some bodies outside through the back door to examine then in the sun light of the heavens making sure they were truly dead.

The important thing to the killers was not to let anyone get away. For some, the work was invigorating; for others, insults made the job easier. I think the perpetrators felt more comfortable insulting and hitting crawlers in rags rather than upright people; because the victims seemed less like them in that position.

When we left the compound, my Uncle Milton decided we would leave town immediately. It was about two p.m. when Uncle Milton, my siblings Eric, Lewis, Catherine, Rita and I started our journey. Uncle Milton was very disturbed and confused after the death of his pregnant wife and son in the rocket attack, but he had to stay strong for us the children because he was the only grown-up we had to lead us out of the war zone. As we wove our way between houses and bodies it became very clear that not everyone beginning that journey had made it to the next destination. Panicked, distressed and crying people were moving through the back roads. We finally reached the cemetery on the edge of the city and made it out of Yekepa.

Seven

WE STARTED WALKING TO GERMAN Camp, the next town over. After four hours of walking, we came to a small village of about thirty small, mud houses which were company facilities already burned down to the ground. We were hungry and hoping there were people who would welcome us and give us some food to eat. Instead, there was nothing but rotten food abandoned in cooking pots in front of every house we came to. Hanging from windows in some mud huts were bodies riddled with bullet holes and half decayed.

Fire blazed through half of the village; smoke blocking the sunlight from coming through. As we escaped through town, we came upon a young lady lying on her stomach not breathing but bleeding perversely from her head. Her baby sat by her side playing in her blood with dry tears tracks on his face. One of the ladies in our group took him as we hurried along. Half an hour after leaving the village we came to a checkpoint control guarded by twelve year old boys with AK-47s loaded with several magazines and sharp knife at the muzzles of their guns.

Human heads, apparently male, were stuck on each end of the gate. The commander was a twenty-year old fellow who came out of the little mud house office. "Small soldiers," he roared, "Tear them up!"

We all lay flat on the ground and furiously begged for our lives. They cocked their guns at us and laughing evilly, told us to roll in the mud.

One of they asked me who I was with, and I said my uncle by pointing at Uncle Milton.

They separated the men from the women. The small soldiers were very cruel. The younger one had a female wig on with human rib bones as a chain around his neck to give him a bizarre fearful look. He rolled his eyes back and forth over the crowd like a hungry lion looking for the perfect prey to devour. Seconds later, he walked past me. My heart rose so fast, I thought it was going to jump out of my chest.

"If anyone moves," he said. "I will kill everyone. Keep your face down." Moments later, he told Mr. Brown, one of my old neighbors, to stand up and dance for him.

I knew this was just the beginning of trouble, because it wasn't pretty. He interrogated Mr. Brown while he danced. "Where you from? What tribe are you?"

Mr. Brown responded with a trembling voice. He accused Mr. Brown of telling a lie. Mr. Brown raised his hands and started pleading for his life, while sobbing, "Please don't kill me, please." Those were the last words I heard coming from Mr. Brown.

The little rebel, with no hesitancy, opened gun fire on Mr. Brown while insulting him. "You dirty Krahn dog."

Mr. Brown ran for his life but did not make it far.

I lifted my head just a little as the small soldier turned his back on us firing at Mr. Brown. I saw at this point Mr. Brown's legs jerking on the unpaved road with blood sprinkling out of his body like water sprinkles on a hot summer day.

"Oh my God," I thought. After this we were more frightened than ever. I managed to hold back my tears and catch my breath before he thought I was a weak person. His twenty-one year old commander came after he heard the gun fire, but did not say a word. Smoking and getting high, he waved his semiautomatic machine gun towards the crowd. "Stand up all of you." In his fearful, roaring voice, he went on to say, "Today is your lucky day. You are all free to go, but do not take any valuables with you."

As we walked away, they pulled their triggers and fired in the air. Everyone starting screaming and stomping on one another because we thought we were being fired on.

Finally the shooting stopped, but it took me a second to realize that I was still alive. Everyone slowly made it out of the bush and back onto the main road where we regrouped and continued our journey. We walked for miles. As the sun was setting set behind the forest line, we came to little village. Only few men welcomed us. Their wives and children ran and hid when strangers approached the village. They took us in. We sat in front of a wood fire as the elders told the horrifying stories of our journey to the villagers.

The next morning, we started our journey to Sanniquellie, the capital of Nimba County, with an escort by one of the local villagers who knew the forest in that region. After hours of walking through the clammy jungle to bypass most checkpoints, we made it to Sanniquellie by night fall.

Eight

TWO MONTHS LATER, I WAS sitting on the old palm tree stump in front of our house in Sanniquellie. My sister Catherine about ten years old at the time was preparing some palm nut soup with some dry monkey meat and cassava; cooking on the other side, she was preparing some fufu, a mushy food made from cassava, in the wooden mortal cooking pot.

My uncle walked slowly back from work, a little contract he had found at the edge of town with the French nonprofit, Medecins sans Frontieres (Doctors without Borders). His bag was on his shoulder and his hairy face was sweating from the hot burning African sun. I had not seen him for a while. My uncle rubbed my head and smiled at me as he came up the steps; he examined my face, and his lips were about to utter something because I had been nutty for days refusing to do my chores; I was missing my parents at this time. Instead, he told us that he would be back and quietly went into the parlor. I held back my tears thinking that I was going to have my butt wiped as usual. I left the front and went to the back of the house.

I had to go and pick up my little sister Rita from this halfway school she got enrolled in which was about ten minutes' walk away from home. When I got to the school, my little sister was in the yard playing nay-four (girls clapping their hands and kicking at the same time) with her friends. A little spitfire, Rita was about eight years old and very pretty. She had light brown skin and very long hair. As soon she saw me, she came running. I knelt as she threw herself on my neck. I was only a year older than Rita and we had a lot of fun together. No matter how much I teased her, we still loved and care for each other. I laughed and told her about the nice soup Catherine was making for lunch as we walked back home under that hot sun.

Before we had time to eat lunch, we heard gunfire from the other side of town. We packed up some food and started to run into hiding again with people crying, "Mama come for me oohs, I go die oohs," and running around all confused.

It was a good thing I had gone to pick Rita up from school early, because now, worried parents' were running back to the school compound to find their kids before going into hiding and this was how many people got killed by stray bullets. A barefooted woman came running and passed us, crying with hands on her head, "My son ooh, my son ooh."

As we exited the village going across the little creek where we used to fetch water; voices cried out, "Yaswaa ooh, maa amu" and "God help us." Parents screamed the names of their sons and daughters. We saw children walking by themselves, naked and running through the crowd.

A baby was left behind by his mother at the back of a house, lying on the cold, muddy ground> He was screaming so hard, we could see his tonsils. My other aunty took him. Today, he is part of the Giplaye family well and alive in Ghana and supported by the family.

Dogs, goats, cows and sheep run among the crowds of people. Behind us all was the sound of the heavy artillery gunfire.

Hundreds of people, including my family, walked for miles and came to Gahnpa, a village on the main road, before getting to Palala. This village was deserted, so we could not stay but kept walking. All that was left in this deserted town were footprints in the mud leading toward the dense forest and the cocoa and rubber farms in between. Some group from that nearby village had run into the rubber farm for hiding as we were there. As we approached, some started stepping out with babies in their hands and man carried their machetes. I heard people in the group chattering in the bushes and whispering that sounded like the cry of little children seeking lost parents. They were tired of walking and the wails of hungry babies' echoes through the rubber plantation as the sun set below the dense forest lines. About ten miles later, we got to Palala to rest for the night and plan for the next petrifying days to come.

We rested for three days in Palala. During that time, Uncle Milton explicitly told the town chief to leave and follow us. I told the little children about the brutal things that I had seen and told them to encourage their parents to abandon their village in peace while they still had time. We knew this village was not safe because it was too close to the major road leading to Gbarnga.

The morning before we left town, we packed some food, mostly plantain, bananas, cassava, dry coconut, oranges and some sweet potatoes. Rice was very difficult to come by. Only higher ranking rebel officers could get rice by killing business owners and looting their stores. As we exited the village that very morning, I turned and waved to the friends I had made during the three days stay. I knew it was probably for the last time; I might not see them again. They stood there watching and waving until we were out of sight.

By noon, we were miles away and already travelled through two tiny barren villages along the way. I could not understand why these town and villages were abandoned but the one where we stayed was not. I decided that those other villages had first hand information that we did not have access to.

Later, we found out that the rebels had now split into two warring factions. While the INPFL and NPFL were continuing their siege on Monrovia, they were making the situation much harder for civilians. Now, we had to deal with two rebel groups. Not only did we have to deal with the killing and torture of government troops and Charles Taylor rebels; now we also had to deal with the General Prince Johnson group that was even more callous and unmerciful.

We scattered out into the night to dig in fields and semi-forest grassland in collection of more food. It was banana season. We ate raw food for a month, hands filthy with mud. Children could no longer drink maternal milk or obtain other nutritious substances from their parents. In most cases, either one or both parents were dead leaving children to extended relatives or at the mercy of total strangers. Hunger and famine spread through the land. Many people, who weren't struck by machetes or stray bullets, were struck down by a deadly weakness during those journeys. In the morning, we woke up and found them, lying beside us, stiffened in their sleep with eyes fixated on the heavens. Without the opportunity to say a word of farewell for them, without a last gift of time, we were unable even to cover them decently. We moved on, letting the dead to bury the dead.

The days went by fast. Often, the sun disappeared behind the clouds and without warning; the rain became to pull from the heavens. The rain falling on the metal roofing of nearby houses sounded like gravel falling from the sky. Little streams of water formed instantaneously causing erosion by finding its way into small rivers at the edge of the towns and villages.

During the evenings, we held assemblies to make rest point suggestions provided the day had not been too chaotic. We could catch hold of no news from anywhere because radio sets no longer blared out, except in the rebels' compounds. Still, we understood by word of mouth that the genocide had spread over the country. All people who could not speak their tribe were considered Krahn, and were to suffer the same fate, to be tortured and beheaded. No one would come to save us anymore. We thought that we would all have to die unless America came to our rescue which did not happen until fifteen years later in 2003 when President George Bush ordered Charles Taylor to step down and leave Liberia.

I heard Kabeh, one elder in the group, and my uncle whispering, saying that because of the split, rebels could be coming from either direction on the main road. We had to branch off and remain off the main roads for some time.

Mr. Varnie suggested that he knew a bypass or shortcut road to Tubman Farm, a farming community off the main road to Monrovia that was still considered safe because the rebel had not made it that far yet. But it would take us days or weeks to get there on foot, and this was long shot. But however, there were smaller villages along the way for rest stops, if they were safe. The Kpelle tribe was nice people, and was very hospitable to strangers. So we regrouped and branched off the main road a few miles away from a little town call Gbloyee.

We took this narrow unpaved path. It was beautiful lined with trees and rubber plantations. The bushes in the distance were green and thick. The floor underneath the plantations was clear of vegetation with decayed leaves covering the dark brown soil on the path. Some of the villages that Mr. Varnie spoke of were completely empty and abandoned by the villagers who had escaped to their farms. Birds had begun building their nests on top of the traditional straws roofing of mud houses, a sign that the inhabitants were long gone by the time we got there.

I no longer concerned myself with thinking about when I would die, since we were going to die anyway. I was only concerned with how they would cut and hack at me and how long it would take for me to die in such pain. I was very frightened by the suffering of others that were hacked and murdered by machetes. On certain nights as the sun returned behind the horizon and the rebels had not killed too many of us that day, we gathered around a bonfire to eat something cooked. On other evenings, we were too dispirited because of deaths from the rebels and stray bullets, dehydration and diarrhea. In the bushes at dawn and the next day, we found more blood in the leaves leading to a trail of mass graves and new corpses that had been dumped over night.

Corpses lying everywhere offended my spirits and scared me to death. We did not dare speak of the dead even though we hurting and infuriated. It was taboo to talk about them amongst ourselves. But the corpses bluntly showed us how our own lives could end at any moment. Our utmost wish in the morning was simply to make it through to the end of the afternoon one more time. I gave myself the courage to live another day, so I and my siblings could someday hopefully be re-united with my parents in the United States of America.

Before getting into a little town called Ganta, we came to a road block. This was the first time I heard the name General Nyeroaga. One of Charles Taylor's leading generals from Libya, he was very wicked. This checkpoint was a mixture of strange men we had never seen before and local boys that we knew from the local community in Nimba County. Between the town of Palala and Ganta, this checkpoint was brutal.

The singing, beating, raping and killing began. It was clear that we would not make it beyond the checkpoint if we could not identify ourselves by speaking the tribe we belonged to. All Krahn would be killed. The legs of the men were assessed for rope marks that would prove they were part of government forces or not. Government forces were on duty for months and had rope burns from keeping their military boots on day and night for so long, which made permanent marking on their legs. Girls as young as nine years old and middle aged women were removed from the group. All young boys and older men were sent to the other side of the barricade. Within minutes, we heard gun shots coming from the back of the little mud house. Men were killed, women raped. Husbands were asked if they wanted to see their wives raped or die. Many saw the wives raped and still got slaughtered with machetes.

The family group a few feet ahead of us was accused of being Krahn. All ten family members were slaughtered. Through the stagnant smell of the dead and the rotting flesh of dead women, men and children, my nose picked up the metallic smell of gunpowder blown on the cool wind across the dusty path. I or any of my family could be next in line for the slaughter. I was terrified and crying.

Many of us were allowed to go through this roadblock so we could be killed at the next checkpoint. We walked for miles, stumbling upon bodies lying along the roadside. The day darkened as the sun returned behind the clouds and heavy wind blew through the deep forest. It began to rain. As the rain water wash over the slaughtered bodies, it turned deep, dusty red in color.

As we approached the next checkpoint, we heard noises from a far distance, the music of guns firing and human out cries. Preceding the checkpoint were mountains of bodies of men, women and their children. Next to some banana bushes were mass graves holding more bodies. These were people who had left Yekepa the day before we did. They were friends and neighbors I knew. To this day, I still have nightmares of seeing my friend Queeyah's body. He was twelve years old from the Krahn tribe. He and his entire family had been murdered before making it to Gbarnga. They had started their journey few days before we did but ended up in one of the mass graves behind the banana bushes at a checkpoint. Everyone was so consumed with preserving his or her own life, there was no such thing as shedding tears or a moment of prayer for the dead.

It was dark and everyone was very tired after walking for hours and days. But the raping and killing did not stop. More girls were taken to be their sex slaves and do their cooking and cleaning against their will. Fathers were murdered because they tried protecting their daughters. Boys became rebels because they were sick and tired seeing their sisters and mothers raped.

My brother Eric joined the rebels' right after my family made it through this checkpoint alive; he claimed that he did it just to protect the family. But this backfired when he had to fight the next battle for a little town of Kanplah and was recaptured. That was the last time the family saw Eric until he managed to escape the April 6, 1996 war. He later joined the family at the Buduburam refugee camp in 1997. He told us his horror stories about how he fought the war and finally escaped without getting killed which he said were a miracle, and I thought so too. As far as the family was concerned, we all thought he was dead.

The family and everyone remained exposed to danger as we began our final hour into Gbarnga. Bullets were flying in the sky like fireworks on the night of New Year's Eve. When we began the journey from Yekepa we were roughly about three thousand people in our small group. But only half of the people in the group made it alive that night into Gbarnba.

CHAPTER

Nine

THE FEW DAYS SPENT IN Gbarnga were terrible.

Before the government troops had left the town of Gbarnga, they looted about every store and took all the local livestock. They also murdered some of the locals who were presumed to be in favor of the revolution or co-conspirators. During which time, the president Doe declare the whole area as enemy territory. It was very difficult to manage this area because the Gio, Mano and Krahn had intermarried in this part of the country for generations. So most Gio men, who married Krahn women, watched their wives and kids got murdered by the rebels. In Grand Gedeh, men and women married to the Gio tribe saw their spouses and children murdered by the government troops which were mostly made up of the Krahn tribe.

After Charles Taylor rebels pushed back the Armed Forces of Liberia (AFL), Gbarnga was filled with the dead. The breeze blowing between the thick green mountainous Forest of Nimba County blew nothing but smells of the decayed bodies and I feared that I or one of my family would became one soon. The evil darkness unleashed from the hearts of our fellow Liberians, brothers and sisters could never be forgotten. The fear I saw in the eyes of men when they slit their throats, was the same fear that fell upon me. But I failed to realize that this was just the beginning of sorrows. I still remember the face of one man as they held a knife to his throat and made him watch while they took turns to raping his wife and then slit his throat after they were finished.

After Gbarnga, we left the main roads and tried to bypass some of the upcoming checkpoints that both rebels and government troops had set up. No one could be trusted, but the group you belonged. We hoped to make it into the town of Suakoko where the only major hospital in the region was located. The weak were left behind with some elders in the group knowing very well that they would not make to the next destination. Other group members died of malaria, starvation, diarrhea and dehydration. By the time we got to Suakoko and Phebe Hospital, it was a little too late. We had hoped to find medical help and some refuge in Suakoko. But the hospital was overcrowded and was more like a cemetery than a place that provided medical care. Children, whose parents had been murdered left their homes in fear and walked miles to the Phebe Medical Center for help.

After weeks of journeying through deep forests and the loss of many lives, I was among the living that made it into a town past Suakoko called Gbatala to enjoy a few weeks of reasonable peace, not real peace, but the reasonable peace of less killing. Approximately six weeks later, we heard that one of Charles Taylor's generals call Jarbah had secured Gbarnga after an epic battle known as "The Fall of Gbarnga." The rebels were moving and capturing fast like there was no such thing known as a Liberian military, the AFL. Government troops took their uniforms and boots off and ran or became part of the general population which made our lives as innocent civilians a whole lot worse. The killing and raping in Gbarnga was not as bad compared to what happened in the towns that were captured initially.

The rebel became to discriminate with their killing moving through the towns of Gbatala and Gbonkonima. I remember their main goal was to capture the town of Totota by the weekend.

A few weeks later Uncle Milton saw one of his friends in Gbatala who offered to give us a ride to the next major city over, called Kakata. "This was such a blessing," my uncle said. "It will save us hundreds of miles in journey on foot." Going past the town of Totota and Salala in a car without walking sounded so good. Especially after months of walking on foot; even better this trip would bring us closer to Monrovia, which had become our main destination to make out of the country.

CHAPTER

Ten

WE STAYED IN KAKATA FOR several months because the town was calm and peaceful. Bars were open to the public, and thousands of people were busy going about their business trying to find food to eat and water to drink. This made us comfortable and gave my family a sense of safety.

One of the major reasons why killing became less was because now everyone knew what the war was about and which group that was being hunted and killed. But it turned more to torture for confessions. Going door to door, the murderers used machetes to decapitate people. Young girls became smarter, and figure out that if they wanted to live, eat, or save their families, and not get gang rape and killed, they must find a rebel boyfriend, the more ruthless the killer the better the boyfriend. This strategy helped some families that had beautiful daughters.

Young men and little boys targeted for child soldiers. Made to watch while their parents were murdered, they were then forced to join the rebels. To make the child soldiers feel brave, the rebels made them drink blood of their enemies and even eat the heart of an enemy. Underage drinking and sexing became the new norm. The child soldiers were given drugs mixed with gun powder to make them feel brave in their killing. They drank and smoked all night, firing the weapons in the sky creating panic and unrest for us. Nobody could sleep because we did not know if it was an attack or some celebration. Yet in the chaos and violence, we managed to make sense of it all. We had to overcome our God given feelings and emotions just to make sense of it all and survive.

I noticed a pattern with the rebels: the more a child soldier kills, the higher he ranked in the revolution, and the more women or girlfriends he had at his disposal. It did not matter if he went to school or not; or knew how to read or write.

While the rape and killing continued at a slower pace, things became more dangerous on a different level. People started to become sick because the drinking water became polluted by dumping corpses into the rivers as a means of easy burial. More lives were lost from cholera and other water borne diseases.

Months after we arrived, the rebels finally attacked Kakata or so it seemed. Catharine was cooking some rice and peanut soup. The soup was done and the rice was almost ready when we heard a single gunshot echo through the town and forest. Catherine ran inside. By then, Rita, Lewis and I were far underneath the bamboo bed. Our uncle ran outside. "What is happening?" he asked.

We stayed in the room waiting for someone to come through that door. I was hoping it would be my uncle. My uncle stood outside trying to determine which rebel group was shooting, like it really mattered. Even though the Prince Johnson boys were more enthusiastic killers than the Charles Taylor boys, but they had one thing in common: "Death to all." A minute later, we heard rapid firing like a .50 caliber gun. This time, my uncle came in and rounded us up from our hide out. He thought it was just the soldiers testing their weapons.

Moments later, the town went deadly silent. We should have known from experience that this was their signature way to attack. I went out outside for the food because I was very hungry. Right that moment, several gunshots went off – which sounded like thunder rolling through the clouds in a hurricane season – and made land fall in Kakata. I dropped the pot of hot soup on the unpaved floor and ran back inside. I did not even realize that my feet were covered in blisters until my sisters pointed, "You will die someday because of your greediness for food" said my sister Catherine. At this point no one was thinking clearly.

In a matter of seconds, people started screaming and running in different directions, pushing and trampling on whoever had fallen on the ground. No one had the time to take anything or anyone for that matter. Everyone just ran to safety. Mothers lost their children again, confusion everywhere; sad cries coincided with the gunshots. Families were separated and left behind everything they had ever work for or believed in their entire lives.

Each gunshot fired seemed to cling to the beat of my heart.

The rebels fired their guns toward the sky, as they shouted and danced in a semi-circle. Before we realized that this was no attack but scare tactics to scare the other rebels away, most of the town population was already in hiding in the forest, swamp and some got seriously injured. Most civilians were terrified and did not return home for days.

After two nights of hiding out in the rubber plantation and running, the men in our group went to assess the town to see if it will be safe to return home. Hours later, they came and told us that it was okay for women and children to return home to nearby villages and the main town of Kakata which Charles Taylor rebels had already taken control of.

Uncle thought it wasn't a good idea to go back to Kakata, but we couldn't stay in the rubber plantation by ourselves either. We followed the group back home. During our journey back, we heard roaring in the distance and everybody walking on that tiny path including me and my uncle dove into the bushes. We all ran fast, but didn't go too far because we found out that it was a cow trapped in the swamp nearby from one of the surrounding villages. My heart was rising fast and I could hear panting everywhere.

As we emerged from the bushes, I noticed an old man running with his arm bleeding. When he stopped he vomited blood and began to cry like a child. I felt sad and terrified and started crying too. My uncle and others went and asked him what the matter was. The women put their arms around him and begged him to stand up. He started to explain by pointing to his house in terror while he was struggling to catch his breath. As we walked him back to the house, he refused to go inside. Crying, he ran back and forth in the front yard. His entire family had been murdered and his daughters raped in their beds with blood everywhere while he was away for a little job during the attack. My whole body went numb; I could not feel the tips of my fingers at that moment because of this terrible scene.

Days later, we traveled from Kakata back to the main road to find our way to Monrovia. When we got to the outer suburbs of Kingsville we found residents on edge because rebels had just passed through. Right in the center of town was the bus and passenger car lot. The rebels had fired on some cars, killing some people, before leaving town to battle for the capital city of Monrovia. The elders in town were removing the bodies and helping the wounded. I saw a man open the driver's side of a taxi cab and a woman fell to the ground. Blood was coming out of her ears. People covered the eyes of their children. In the back of the car were more dead bodies, two girls. One of the girls had a baby boy on her lap that also got shot. Their blood was seeping from corners of the car. I wanted to faint, but ran to the side and threw up everything that I ate that morning for breakfast.

The rebel forces got into their vehicles and drove away firing into the sky.

Everyone tried to console one another. For a few seconds at least, women embraced one another and cried together. They, at least, had time to bury their loved ones. It was a sad day. The air was humid, the wind stopped moving and day light seemed to fade away quickly. At sun set, more people came through Kingsville from other terrorized small villages in the area. One man carried his dead daughter looking for help or a hospital. Either he did not know his little girl was dead, or he was in denial. The father was soaked in his daughter's blood, and as he ran, he kept yelling, "I will get you to the hospital, my child, and everything will be fine."

A group of men and women who had been pierced by stray bullets came running next. Blood was running out of their ears and one of the men had his hand chopped off for defying the rebels. He was lucky his life was spared because he was the son of a well-known town chief. All the villagers that came running had open wounds caused by bullets, burns, machetes and other sharp objects. Their skin and broken limbs hung down from their bodies still oozing fresh blood and other bodily fluids. Some of them didn't even notice that they were wounded until they stopped at a mid-way tent clinic of Red Cross relief workers that had just started arriving from Monrovia.

One sign of the hopelessness of our situation had been that there were no viable clinics or hospitals open. We had heard that the American Red Cross had been making its way into the combat zone but was terrorized by the rebels, so the mission had been aborted.

Some fainted or vomited in the town square. I felt sick to my stomach and terrified just from seeing these villagers arrived in such condition. This brought back bad memories from our first attack in my various journeys, I became anxious and my adrenalin started to rise, but Uncle Milton thought it was wise for the family to stay hoping that we could get some medical and international help from the American Red Cross if the rebels were to attack.

The last casualty that I saw that evening was a woman who carried her baby on her back and her belongings on her head. Blood was running down her legs and dripping behind her. Her two little sons trailed after her. One was about my age at the time, nine-years-old, and the other one was maybe twelve-years-old. The child on her back had been dead for hours and she had not noticed because they were running furiously for their lives. Her husband was on the farm with the older son when this attack happened. She ran from home with her boys hoping their lives would be spared.

The Red Cross lady took the baby from the mother's back to treat his wounds. It was a baby boy. His eyes were still open with the innocent look of infanthood interrupted by the tragedy of war. His brothers thought he was sleeping through all the chaos and violence the whole time. They had no clue that their little brother had passed on.

After her treatment, the mother asked for her baby, and the Red Cross woman took a deep breath while she hesitantly gave her the bad news. The woman blacked out and fell to the floor. The lady sat with her in panic until she came to herself. The woman asked to see her baby and then, in a trembling voice, "What happened, God what happened?" The Red Cross employee consoled her and escorted her to see the dead child. She took her dead child and tightly clung to the dead baby boy while she rocked him back and forth sobbing.

I had left my family and walked over to her tent to see what was happening. I later made friends with her other two boys. We ran in the Red Cross compound the next day as if nothing happened the day before, playing soccer with a green grapefruit as a soccer ball. But the memory of their mother sobbing as she held on to their little brother would be my nightmare for the next few days until another one came along.

Eleven

AS WE LEFT KINGSVILLE DAYS later on our journey to Mount Barclay, I wondered how I would explain the war to my parents or maybe children of my own someday if I was lucky enough to be alive. I asked my uncle what the war was really about.

He said, "The rebels said they are freedom fighters. They have come to liberate us from the corrupt Doe regime."

"But uncle, they are shooting more innocent civilians, women and children, than the people of the corrupt Doe regime. Who will they govern when the war is over, if the rebels are killing us all?"

My uncle smiled at me. "No matter what they do, or how many of us they kill, they cannot murder everyone. We will see it through the end. Don't worry my son." We continued walking as I held on to my little sister Rita's hand and my uncle carried my little brother Lewis on his back.

Months of starvation and torture from the rebel forces had turned us into walking skeletons through these journeys. I saw very sad faces, friends that I once knew who came from wealthy families. It no longer mattered; the smell of sorrow was in every household. Everybody turned to God, praying and worshiping for their life to be spared by the rebels.

There were rumors in the air that the government forces were coming back with re-enforcement to retake all the cities we had passed through already under the rebels' control. So at three a.m., we had taken everything we had left of value and continued our journey to Monrovia. The walking started, but it was dead silence in the bush. Anything could happen to us at any moment, because nowhere was safe. There were ambushes everywhere, mothers with babies were ordered to keep their breasts in the baby's mouth at all times to prevent that baby from crying or making any noise.

Out of nowhere, the government troops had rounded up re-enforcements to take back Kakata. We were stuck in the middle and got driven back into the forest between Kingsville and Kakata.

Uncle Milton decided to return to Kakata. It would take some time for the government troops to make it there. For this reason, Kakata was the only safe direction to go. We took the back roads and stayed off the main roads, which were nothing but deep dark forest crawling with reptiles, monkeys and wild cats. As the government advanced, everyone was running for their lives and taking cover like small, scared children. The sounds from the artillery and explosives were all around us. I was very frantic but my adrenalin rush was not enough to slow me down or make me move any faster. We journeyed in silence, afraid and terrified that our voices could attract attention or awake an ambush. At one point we came upon a village that was set on fire. So we decided to go around the village thinking that the killers might still be there. On the outskirts of the village, we came upon rotting bodies, mostly men and women. Their children were taken; we knew it was the government troops because their motto was save all children.

We all stood and cried and prayed. Knowing we were not safe in this area, we needed to find our way back to the main road which was at least twenty-five kilometer journey on foot. The strong carried the weak, kids and old people, as we found our way back to the main road. Hours later, a few miles away from the main road, we had had enough walking for that day. The night was falling.

We made a fire and slept that night while the men took rotation keeping watch for killers, snakes and wild animals. As the day broke, we heard voices, and then suddenly we heard, Paw! Paw!!!!! Heavy artillery fire. Everyone took cover. Later, a few men went ahead of the group to spy on the main road. We were close to Charles Taylor's camp and had nowhere else to run. We could not go back to where we came from after what we saw the day before. And we believed the rebels were more likely to spare our lives than the government soldiers. The government soldiers were killing all men and boys because the rebels wore civilian clothes. So it was hard to distinguish the rebels from the civilians.

We all agree to go into the Charles Taylor's rebel camp. But we forgot that there were layers of ambushes around the camp. As we came closer, armed men surrounded us. We attempted dashing under the bushes to hide, but it was too late. Boy soldiers were everywhere. They accused us of spying for their enemies, and committing various crimes. Separating the men and boys from the women, they beat men and boys severely while they searched the women harshly. We were accused of being new recruits in the government army and the only way we could prove this wrong was to join in the next fight.

The beating and torture continued while they took the females in their house. Older men's hands were tied to their back. We boys were told to walk in circles non-stop, from the rising of the sun until it set. The rain came and got us wet; the sun came and dried us up. We begged for food and water, but they only gave us water. Later, their commander came and took three men. These men were accused of being from a Mandingo tribe. They had started killing Mandingo tribe members because they were regarded as non-citizens in Liberia until Doe's regime. For this reason, the Mandingo tribe was very loyal to the Doe government. Charles Taylor had ordered his rebels to exterminate all Mandingoes. Kamarah, Jumali and Artah were murdered as we watched.

These men sensed that their time left to live was seconds to minutes. Their wives begged the rebels to let their husbands go, but instead they were held at gun point to watch the murders. These men started fighting the rebels while trying to escape, but they could not do much because their hands were tied. A child soldier call Little Eagle used the machete to detach their arms from their bodies. Two other child soldiers joined Little Eagle and slit the throats of these three men who had protected us for days through those horrifying journey. These men's heads rolled off their bodies like soccer balls rolling on the lawn.

We all started praying and begging for our lives. What were these boys going to do to us after what they did to our friends? Their commander came out after raping one of the young girls. He said since we were not Mandingoes, we should be put in prison. But it was too late for our friends that got beheaded. All the men were put into jail. I heard chuckling from rebels, who whispered, "We shall have fun tonight. New girls are here."

The Valley of Dry Bones

The jail was a valley of mass graves. It was an old mining site, manmade craters as deep as 50 to 100 feet deep from mining gold and diamonds in the middle of the forest surrounded by armed men. The scene around us was terrible, full of dry human bones and skulls. I became to think we will be dead anyways. Every morning, we were brought outside and offered some green cassava leaves to eat. A few days later, we were taken to another place in the deep forest. Here they told us we had to become rebels or remain in prison. This thought was quite wild, because I witnessed these guys disregard for human life and how they raped little girls and women old enough to be their mothers. They made us drink from human skulls to make us feel brave, but my uncle refused to join. So they beat us more and made us bury the dead bodies. This torture continued for several days before we were set free.

The new guard on duty for the next rotation knew my uncle from school from his high school days and was able to convince his commanding officer that we posed no threat to their mission.

We started walking back to Kakata to find Catherine, Rita and Lewis and the rest of the women in the group. The women were led by a lady call Mama Yaah who was the elderly woman in the group. My feet felt heavy; I was afraid of the road. Clouds floated above the distant mountains and haze loomed over the trees on the mountain tops. Birds sang from tree tops; crickets and frogs chirped from the swampier valley. But the chills were still crawling over my body after that stay among the dead bodies.

I had been tempted to join the rebels just to be free of all these torture. Most children, who became orphans or were separated from their parents voluntary, became child soldiers just to be protected by the rebels. I was forturnate enough to have my uncle around for such protection. Even though we got beaten and tortured on most occasions, it was better than becoming a child soldier. Most children never had this option.

My brother Eric was influenced to become a child soldier because of peer pressure. He was fourteen years old at the time, but other children signed up as young as eight and nine years of age. Rebels had easy access to food and protection and other basic necessities by means of using their weapons to intimidate other citizens and taking whatever they wanted.

My uncle was worried about the girls, Catherine and Rita, who were then staying with the older women in our group somewhere in the village. Hours later, we arrived safely after being roughed up at some of the checkpoints along the way. Catherine and Rita were safe with Mama Yaah, the elder woman in the group. I was very worried about my sisters, most especially Catherine, who was older. During this period of the war, young girls were becoming most useful for reconnaissance missions because they could go through the crowd unsuspected. Also, little girls as young as nine years old were being used as bush wives or rewarded to rebel leaders who killed the most people. But most of them were raped over and over again and taken for sex slaves in the jungle. This practice would continue to grow as the rebels attacked more towns and villages burning every house in their path, murdering families and taking their daughters.

To protect Catherine from been raped, Mama Yaah used a pocket knife and cut her hair off her head. Then she dressed her in boys clothing making her to look like a little boy. This trick was able to spare Catherine's life at most checkpoints.

When Uncle Milton and I arrived back to the house after our release from the valley of dry bones, we were relieved to be free from the nights of torture, but sad because the air in the town still smelled of fresh blood and decayed bodies; the older men sat in front of their houses on wooden benches with terror in their eyes afraid of what would happen next. Sporadic flames of cooking smoke graced the heaven from backyards owned by rebels; the rest of the town was starving and petrified.

A day later uncle Milton and I decided to go and look for food in the neighborhood; right after we turned the corner to take a foot path to where Catherine and Rita were staying, we ran into a checkpoint next to the open cement sewer line leading into the river downstream. The open sewer was blocked with bodies that had missing legs, arms or heads. Gut spilled out of some bodies where bullet holes had torn into stomachs. Brain matter oozed through noses and ears. Vultures and flies filled the air attracted to the pools of blood and decaying bodies. Some used their AK-47s to shoot at the vultures for their next barbecue meal.

They pointed their guns and stopped us. My uncle explained who we were. They had us wait until more groups of people arrived at the checkpoint. Finally, they ordered all men to use some rusty wheelbarrows they had next to the decaying bodies to remove the corpses so the water could start flowing again. They were merciful enough to allow me sit with the women on the other side of the checkpoint. My heart pounded faster as I bowed my head to the ground sitting on a big rock facing the bush. I became brave for a little while and lifted my head to see my uncle and the others pull the bodies out of the sewer line. I saw blood dripping from the wheelbarrow and arms and legs dangling held in place by their pants and shirts. The flies had a feeding frenzy.

One of the child soldiers about my age came over to me and told me to join the men take the bodies to the cemetery. I did not hesitate. When we arrived at the cemetery, I struggled to lift the body from the wheelbarrow. It felt as if the body were resisting. I carried it in my arms, looking for a suitable place to bury it in an open grave somewhere in the cemetery. My whole body ached and I couldn't lift a foot without a rush of pain shooting down from the top of my head through my spine to the soles of my feet. I collapsed on the ground, holding the body in my arms. It was a little girl. Blood began to seep through the white bed sheet covering the body. Setting the body on the ground, I start to start to unwrap it, beginning from the head and working down to the feet. When I got to her waist I noticed that she had no underwear on and there was more blood. They had raped and tortured her before killing her.

One bullet had gone through her lift eye and exited behind her right ear, making a big hole on exit. I ran into the old church in the cemetery to find a shovel, did not find any. I lay on the floor in the church sweating for a few minutes looking at the cross at the upper back wall with sunlight shining through the Jesus image on the cross. Being in the church that moment brought back painful memories of the incident that happened at the Assembly of God Church in Nimba County. A pain ran through my spine as I lifted myself off the floor. I ran through the back door and there was a casket in a small room with a body in it still waiting for viewing. Everyone one had run for their lives when the rebels attacked and they had left the body.

I was able to find my way home alive. I met my uncle and sisters sitting in front of the house worried sick about me when they heard the gunfire earlier that day on the other side of town. My uncle did not even know that I was asked to join the men get rid of the bodies after the rebels stopped us at the checkpoint. He thought they had let me go and I would be waiting for him with my sisters at the house.

My sister Catherine hugged me and clung to my body tightly. They did not want to let go of me. I was grounded for days as a punishment by my uncle because he did not believe me when I told him I was asked to help remove the bodies after he left.

There was gunfire across town that afternoon. My uncle later explained that he was out looking for food for us to eat when he saw some small soldiers who had just come from the battle field with looted items. He said, "They had just come from attacking a town call Harbel where the big Firestone rubber plant is located." This was rich looting for the rebels because the Firestone Rubber Company is one of the biggest and richest private operating companies in the United States of America with their present in Liberia. It was known as the Holy Grail of the war after the capital, Monrovia. The small soldiers came back with ammunitions, clothes, young girls and food. They had burned to the ground every village and town along the way back home, and now one group opened fire on the other group because the looted items were not shared fairly."

Several innocent people died including some of the girls they kidnapped and brought with them from Harbel. Hundreds of people in the town square got injured critically and later died at home or at the local clinic. The bodies consisted of many young boys and girls.

My uncle said, "Nowhere is safe my children. That is why I want you kids to stay at home until I can find a way to safely get us out of here."

Catherine was even more scared because any journey we made outside our hiding zone put her at risk of rape or being taken as one of the rebels bush wives. Some nights Catherine stayed up all night sobbing under her bed sheet out of fear.

At some of the checkpoints, when the women were separated from their families, some of the teenage girls and adult women were gang raped while their men and boys were being tortured on the other end. But these women and girls would not tell their husbands or families because of the fear of their husbands leaving them or being outcast by society.

On our most recent journey during the separation of the group, she had witnessed a teenage girl in her group being raped so badly and repeatedly slapped by her rapists over and over as she struggled. Catherine said, "The last thing I saw she fought the young rebel and was punching and fighting in response to the excruciating pain she was feeling. She did not mean to punch the guy, but the rebel saw it as disrespect. He grabbed a knife from his boot and stabbed her in her stomach over and over again until she stopped moving under him. After he walked out of the room, Mama Yaah went over and held her hands. Seconds later, she died with blood over her whole body, her innocent eyes open fixated toward the ceiling." Catherine refused to embark on any more journeys after this incident. She locked herself up in a room whenever she heard Uncle Milton talk about another journey to hid for safety.

Twelve

AT NIGHT, THE TOWN WAS completely silent after the sound of gunfire across town during the day. More than half of the population had escaped town and run to their farms in the forest to be in hiding. With the absence of so many people, the town looked like a ghost town. Normally at night children will play and dance in moon light while old folks sat at bon fire and told stories. But now, everyone remained indoors.

Weeks went by and people started coming out of hiding. Their physical presence rejuvenated the town. Some mid-way schools reopened and food items started flowing from other towns nearby.

It was the harvest season, but money was hard to come by because the rebels looted it all. So the locals developed an exchange system that the rebels did not understand. Villagers from the towns of Wong, Zwiota and Sanoyie came to town every market day with fresh crops like pepper, rice, monkey and deer meat to trade for salt, seasonings, flip flops, used clothes, flash lights, batteries, etc. This method of exchange was really working for the locals, until the rebels figured it out and started ambushing the villagers on the mornings of market day, beating them up, and taking away their crops. This scared the villagers away and we had to find a way to sneak into the forest and find these villages for food.

One gorgeous morning at sunrise, a messenger came into the Red Cross compound at Kingsville to deliver a message that Prince Johnson rebels had just attacked some towns and villages a couple of miles away. Somehow, this news echoed across town and created total panic. Residents starting packing belongings and what they could carry; by noon, the majority of the town's population had quietly gone back into the forest to their previous hide out locations.

Charles Taylor rebels began getting ready for the incoming attack when they got the news. They started testing their weapons by firing into the air. This created more chaos for the remaining residents. Early that morning, my uncle said we had to follow some groups that were taking the main road to the Kakata City again. This was a gutsy and risky move. But he explained it would get us closer to our destination than running into the forest to hide out.

Another Escape Attempt to Monrovia

We started our journey to Monrovia on foot. The odor in the air was musty. Everyone was sweaty, dirty, thirsty and hungry. Many of us would die off and be left by the road side by family and friends before we got to Monrovia. Knowing the impending danger, everybody was under pressure to perform well and make it alive to the capital. Some families carried their weak in a wheelbarrow.

Change came quickly between night and day. The darkness swiftly rolled back, allowing the sunrise to shine through the forest. We heard some chattering from a distance, so we all ran into the bushes for cover. A group of boys walked by on the path carrying AK-47s and machetes. They were all wearing red T-shirts and black jeans. The group in the front was humming and the last group in the back was mumbling something which was very difficult to understand. I heard the last one say, "Death to all when we arrive." They were going in the direction of a small village near Kakata.

After these men were long gone, the men leading our group whispered for everyone to come out, that it was safe. People started coming out sporadically, breathing heavily. My hands and legs were trembling uncontrollably as we moved along the path. A young woman came out with her hands on her head crying because her baby was not waking up after he fell to sleep. She said, "He was crying when we took cover as the bad men were approaching. I tried to breastfeed but he would not stop crying, so I held my hands to his face and he stopped crying and fell to sleep shortly after he stopped crying. But now he is not waking up. Please somebody help, please!!" The toddler had died from suffocation. We all gathered around her, the other women were terrified and suggested that we take the baby to the next village and give him a proper burial. But the men in the group refused, because this would draw more attention to the group. So they buried the body in the forest before we started our journey. He was an eight month old boy and his name was Coolah.

Halfway through our journey to the next town, the dead boy's mother, Sarah, became very weak and ill. She had been sobbing the entire way and had refused to eat or drink anything at all. She was dehydrated and had diarrhea on top of all this, so she became very weak to the point that the men in the group made a wooden stretcher to carry her in. She was vomiting and saying words about her dead son, which did not make any sense. Her brother poured some water in her month from the calabash. She was hallucinating, but others thought she was seeing the ghost of her son.

It was a gloomy day and the sun was hot like an oven when we arrived at this very crowded town. I was surprised that this town was so lively. The people were very noisy. Children were running around and playing while adults sat in front their houses playing music loudly from the open stereo players. I asked my uncle "Is the war over now?"

"No son, it must be a market day."

We walked through the crowd quickly trying to find a clinic for the dead boy's mom, as people hesitantly waved to us. We later found some old man who helped us located the local nurse in the town and brought the weak young lady into her backyard. The women followed the nurse into the backyard as she carried a bucket of cold water to sprinkle over Sarah. The men sat quietly in the front pouch of the house. We the kids joined the other kids running and playing under the mango trees. Hours later, the men and women started gathering on the front pouch. Then, I saw them whispering into one another ears. Sarah's brother began to cry and ran behind the house. Everyone else was crying too.

I felt light headed and sat on the tree stump. My legs were trembling and my hands shaking; my heart rate began to rise heavily and I became diaphoretic.

Some women went into the backyard while the others were consoling Sarah's brother. They prepared her body for burial that same day. Sarah's body was placed in a wooden coffin made by the men and set on the table underneath the mango tree for viewing. As the day went by Sarah's friends and traveling companions stood by her coffin and expressed their feelings about the death of her son and now her death. Her brother said he and Sarah were the only family living. He wondered what would happen to him without his big sister Sarah. By sunset, the men stood up and carried Sarah's coffin through the town to the cemetery.

After days of traveling on foot and the loss of hundreds of lives, we made it into the capital Monrovia. Uncle Milton was able to find an old friend's house when we entered the city. I called the friend, Uncle Joe. Uncle Joe allowed us to stay at his place until the unrest was over. There was so much commotion in the city because people were leaving the country by airplane, cars and ships if they had the money. There was chaos and unrest in the entire city. In those depressing times, only a few individuals had radio, but everybody was interested to know what was happening in the country. My uncle went to a nearby Lebanese business to listen to the morning news. When he came back to Uncle Joe's house, he repeated what he had heard, leaving the bad news out so we wouldn't worry.

At night we all gathered by the bon fire on a long wooden bench and listened to Uncle Milton tell stories. He narrated to us in a loud, distinctive voice and took on roles like in a Shakespeare play. While he was singing the songs of the stories, we would all join in while complete darkness fell. Looking back, his stories of hope, peace and survival were the only light in the midst of that chaotic and endless darkness. Today I tell my stories to my sons, Hanstin and Akais, just to tell them how blessed they are. Even though yesterday is gone and the deep wounds of yesterday are healed, the scars remain and continue to remind me of my darkest moments in life. I have come to understood that many people would be unable to comprehend the full scope of this horror I am trying to explain in this book. But I also understood that any human deeds that were so utterly evil and demonic were already done, and all did eventually happened in my life.

In Monrovia, things that were looted from the outskirts of the city were sold at flea markets. At one of these markets, Johnson Markets, the slogan was, "Buy your own thing," and they were serious about this. You could literally find your belongings that were looted from your house, including family portraits at these flea markets. If you wanted them back, you would have to buy them back at inflated prices. I remember a man who had lost his entire family in the fall of Gbarnga. The only remembrance he had left of his wife and children was a black and white picture in this beautiful Italian art frame. He was very excited to see this picture at one of those "buy our own thing" flea markets in Monrovia.

He said to the kid selling this portrait, "My son, this is me and my family." He pointed to himself in the picture.

The small soldier said, "Are you calling me a thief?"

"No, No, No," the old man said, "Just saying, it will be good if I can have it back, because my family is dead, and this will be the only thing I will have to remember them by."

The kid said, "Well, pay some money now to have it."

The old man did not have any money but continued to beg for the portrait because he really wanted it. The next thing I heard was the AK-47 going off, everyone went hiding. This kid used gun butt of the AK-47 to beat the old man up beyond recognition while the old man pleaded for his life. No one wanted to get killed. As a result, we all went about our business until this old man was set free at the mercy of the twelve-year-old rebel. He suffered broken bones in his face, ribs, and arm. He died of his injuries later the following day.

Thirteen

AS THE GOVERNMENT TROOPS WENT from Monrovia to do battle in nearby towns and villages, they came home with children after murdering and slaughtering their parents. These war orphans were given out for adoption. But later in the process the commanding generals had the impression that these children would grow up someday and take revenge for their parents and bloodline. So one hostile and fearful morning, we heard gunshots firing in a part of the city called Red-light. Red-light was one of the city's busiest market places. We became very distressed, scared and panicky.

My uncle tremulously locked Rita, Lewis, Catherine and me in Uncle Joe's house and went to find out. He later came back devastated and disconsolate. He sorrowfully told us that a truck load of orphans brought from the war zone were murdered by dumping them into the well. They did this even though there were women, churches and families waiting to adopt these kids. Everyone was grieving and alarmed. This moment would mark the beginning of unrest in Monrovia.

In the middle of the night, there was no light. The power supply to the whole city was cut off. My siblings and I slept in a one bedroom cage. The room was hot and humid. One night, I discovered tiny, sweating hands shaking underneath the covers. It was my baby brother, five year old little Lewis, curled up in a fetal position terrified from the extreme horror he had experienced and witnessed through all those torturous journeys. He was having a nightmare, thinking that the rebels were going to kill us that night and throw him in the well like the government militia did to the other children. I held him as we fell to sleep.

The next day was also hot and humid. As morning advanced, the heated air grew furiously hotter; the sun became red and large very quickly. I noticed Lewis was still having panic attacks from the aftermath of nightmares he had during the night. He followed me around; afraid of everything that moved, and jumps at every sound around the house.

Life in Monrovia

A few weeks later, rebel leader Prince Johnson and his rebels launched an attack on Monrovia. On my way back home from the National Port Authority, known as Freeport, I heard screams and shouts from nearby that got progressively louder. Gunshots and explosions rocked the ground I was walking on as I crept into the center of the city. There was no turning back because I had to make home. If I didn't, I would lose my family for good. I was sure Uncle Milton would have found a hiding place for Rita, Catherine and Lewis. But they would all be worried about me.

Debris from explosions was landing closer and closer around me. I saw people running in one direction and decided to join the group. As I ran away from the gunfire direction, a grenade exploded near by accompanied by the sound of machine guns and a series of small explosions. Diving into a pile of dirt, I was momentarily deaf. Minutes later, I began to crawl toward a burnt concrete house nearby through the mix of metallic bullet shells, freshly spewed blood, body parts and debris splattered all over the ground. In the distance, a mother and child collapsed as I crawled into the building to take cover.

I noticed blood on my left leg and wrist. This was too warm to be somebody else's. I had huge cuts that were bleeding profusely. I took off my shirt, tore it into pieces, and wrapped up my wounds to avoid bleeding to death.

For almost an hour, I took cover at the back of the house. The pain was so unbearable that I started screaming and shouting for help. There was no response but sounds of explosions and gunfire. The smell of gunpowder filled the air around me. I was scared, but my pain and the warm blood oozing through my cloth give me a sense of urgency and the strength to get up and keep moving to the next location for help.

I made my way out between houses and containers left along the road. There were burnt houses everywhere. Victims had fought fiercely to free themselves from burning houses only to die a painful death outside with no help in sight. They lay on the ground or ran to muddy puddles to quench the fire on their bodies. I ran with a group of strangers towards a bunch of empty forty-foot containers from the Freeport abandoned in the heat of the fighting. This was safer that running into a house. With no warning what so ever, a heavy storm clouds then began rolling overhead and the high pitch rumble of thunder from the stormy cloud terrifies me even more. At the first few flashes of lightning, I looked up from the corner of an abandoned mud house with the strolls roofing completely gone, I saw nothing but bullets and rockets electrified that skies in the mix of flashing lightning.

As I escaped from the back of the unroofed mud house I saw a little girl lost from her parents. She was so terrified; she had curled up in fetal position at the back of a house.

She was about five years old. I grasped her by the hand and we ran between the containers together. The black and white smoke blanketed the sky above us as if the clouds had fallen close to earth. The sun became dark as the gunshots grew louder like a thundering rain. We were in the container for about two hours until the gunfire ceased. After that, we got out and started running finding our way out of Freeport, Liberia's main commercial port facility in Monrovia. I still held onto the little girl's hand because I could not leave her in the container by herself. As we ran between the narrow corridors and muddy narrow paths, we passed a house completely burnt except for the concrete frame standing with the burnt bodies of a mother and child lying at the base of the window. The mother's burnt hands still held her baby's body tightly. Some wrist and arm bones were still visible. I covered the little girl's eyes as we ran past these corpses and made our way to an American Red Cross station.

The Red Cross took the little girl's picture and placed it on the bulletin board. At the Red Cross Station, wounded people lay all over the place waiting to be treated for burns and bullet wounds. I myself suffered some injuries caused by a rocket explosion nearby and was treated but the scars are still largely visible. I slept at the Red Cross center where some hot meals were provided and found my way home the next morning after the fighting cooled off. On my way home, smoke still loomed in the skies from burning cars and houses. The streets were very fearful with corpses everywhere. Expect there was no gunfire; the rebel had retreated to their respective territories.

About a week later, there was no food or access to clean drinking water. We seemed likely to starve, but a group of boys from the neighborhood came by from the Freeport with some bags of rice and vegetable oil that they had taken from looted containers and warehouses in the area. They asked me to follow them on their next trip, and I agreed. My uncle was not home, so I snuck out through the back window and followed those boys to the Freeport because I was hungry and needed food for me and the family.

We saw an unattended container right outside the exit of the Freeport. It was open but had a corpse lying around. I told those guys that this was a trap. There were rockets flying overhead launching into the port. Fighting had intensified that morning for some reason. We got some bags of rice and beans out and decided to leave the area really quick. As we were running between the houses, we heard gunshots and people screaming and crying from a distance. We dropped the bag of rice and began running. I did manage to put little bits of rice in my pockets and was eating that raw whenever I got hungry.

I heard a big boom behind me coming from the Freeport direction. I turned and saw thick blue-black smoke rising from the port. Following the smoke were sparks and then flames leapt into the air like an atomic bomb his exploded in that area. We could feel the heat wave from miles away. Gunshots followed. We dove into the road side bushes between the houses and listened to the artillery fire on and on, while men and women screamed in the distance and children wailed from nearby house. The sound of the guns and artillery was very powerful and loud, but the cries of the children were more compelling and caused me excruciating pain because it evoked the memory of the death of my little brother.

We got out of the bushes and ran in different directions to find our way home. I ran so fast and didn't even feel my legs. I got home sweating because of the running and heat, and met my uncle sitting on the pouch very angry at me. I got grounded for days after some serious spanking too. Later on during the day, we got the news that the president was captured at Freeport, and that was what the fighting was all about early that morning.

Everybody's lives were in shambles at this point; chaos was everywhere. There were mass exoduses in every region of Liberia. ECOWAS had attempted to persuade Doe to resign and go into exile. Besieged in his mansion, he had refused. While making a brief trip out of the Executive Mansion to ECOMOG Headquarters, Doe was captured by Johnson on September 9, 1990, and tortured before being killed. The spectacle was videotaped and seen on news reports around the world. When the gunshots finally ceased, tens of thousands of corpses covered the streets of Monrovia, and the entire city was deadly silent, I mean soundless for a while.

By the end of 1990, a civil war was raging. Taylor's NPFL controlled much of the country, while Johnson had taken most of the capital, Monrovia. Peace was still far off as both Taylor and Johnson claimed power. The Interim Government of National Unity was formed In November 1990. ECOWAS invited the principal Liberian players to meet in Banjul, Gambia to form a government of national unity. The negotiated settlement established the Interim Government of National Unity (IGNU), led by Dr. Amos Sawyer, leader of the LPP. Bishop Ronald Diggs of the Liberian Council of Churches became vice president. However, Taylor's NPFL refused to attend the conference.

Within days, hostilities resumed. ECOMOG was reinforced in order to protect the interim government. Dr. Sawyer was able to establish his authority over most of Monrovia, but the rest of Liberia was in the hands of various factions of the NPFL or of local gangs. Fighting intensified as the remnants of the Doe regime pushed for a last stand off to maintain their position at the Executive Mansion. My uncle, siblings and I were living around the Freeport, where president Doe got captured. The fighting in this area was fierce, rockets launching through the sky and hitting homes in and around the area. Thousands were killed while thousands more were injured.

Fourteen

ABOUT SIX MONTHS LATER, WE were in turmoil again. The United Liberation Movement of Liberia for Democracy (ULIMO) was formed in June 1991 by supporters of the late President Samuel Doe and former Armed Forces of Liberia (AFL) fighters who had taken refuge in Guinea and Sierra Leone after the capture and murder of President Doe. It was led by Raleigh Seekie, a deputy Minister of Finance in the Doe government. After fighting alongside the Sierra Leonean army against the Revolutionary United Front (RUF), ULIMO forces entered western Liberia in September 1991. The group scored significant gains in areas held by another rebel group, the National Patriotic Front of Liberia (NPFL), notably around the diamond mining areas of Lofa and Bomi counties. This attack sent us into hiding once again and the war was far from over. It would last for another thirteen years.

From its outset, ULIMO was beset with internal divisions and the group effectively broke into two separate militias, ULIMO-J, an ethnic Krahn faction led by General Roosevelt Johnson and ULIMO-K, a Mandingo-based faction led by Alhaji G.V. Kromah. This separation led to the senseless murder of innocent Liberians from all sixteen ethnic groups in the country. Families got destroyed because brothers fought each other as one brother was ULIMO-J and the other was ULIMO-. This was how senseless the war was, now come to think of it.

The Interim Government of National Unity (IGNU) headed by Dr. Sawyer – now assistant professor at Indiana State University – had the broad support of Prince Johnson but not Charles Taylor who launched new attacks on Monrovia in 1992. This attack sent us running for our lives again and caused a mass exodus of starving, wounded people to neighboring countries like the Ivory Coast, Sierra Leone, Ghana and Guinea as refugees. But ECOMOG reinforced the city and negotiated a treaty between the NPFL, Prince Johnson and Doe's remaining supporters (known as the United Liberation Movement of Liberia for Democracy or ULIMO). The treaty was known as the Cotonou Peace Agreement. A coalition government was formed again in August 1993. For about three years there was peace - until April 6, 1996.

Taylor and his National Patriotic Front rebels had gained the support of many Liberians when they reached the outskirts of Monrovia and clashed with the forces of Prince Johnson.

People started to leave the capital. Some with money boarded the first ship to Ghana, while others took buses and cars to Sierra Leone. We were frightened because we did not have enough money to leave the country. But my uncle suggested that we travel to Sinoe County, the southern-eastern part of the country to join extended family members in their village in the midst of the jungle. My grandfather from my father's side of the family had come from this village. We apprehensively went to the bus station and boarded a truck with other petrified refugees to start another unknown journey. I was now eleven years old

After four days and four nights of road travel and hundreds of checkpoints, we arrived in the south-eastern region of the country which was still under the control of government forces. But the atmosphere was far from peaceful. There were rumors in the communities there that the rebels were fast advancing. That they now controlled about seventy percent of the country was not reassuring. People were moving all around like a lost herd of cattle. They carried their belongings on their heads and children on their backs. More kids trotted behind them while their dads said, "Hurry, hurry." Everyone could tell you about where they came from, but had no idea where they were going.

Our journey was not yet over; my family had to walk on foot for days to get to the village in the south-eastern region of Liberia. On our way, we stopped to rest for a while. Climbing up steep mountains was not that easy, especially for my aunt and uncle who were in their late thirties to forties. The single path road was rocky and hard to traverse. I turned around to look when we rested half way on the hill top. Around us was a beautiful valley surrounded by mountains on both sides. As the wind blew through the deep forest, the top of the canopy danced in the direction on the wind. Monkeys swung from one tree branch to the next. Very beautiful and different animal species also played under the trees.

There was a river at the base of the mountain when we descended the other side. This river was shallow, so clean and clear that I could see the fish swimming through. I said to myself, all this beauty makes this suffering and long journey worthwhile.

Local villagers were making this walk with us. This was a different journey from the others we had taken. We did not feel pressure or terrified. Instead, I felt alive, cheerful, and grateful to be making it this far. Here I was coming from valley of dry bones and human skulls, into a real paradise of

Mother Nature. No photograph from my elementary text had shown me anything like this. As we travelled through, I felt the power, majesty, energy and jubilance of the rain forest.

Stopping to rest at little towns along the way, we walked from rainforest to the next. The air was so fresh, clean and so heavy with oxygen and humidity that it was almost as tangible. During short rests on the river banks, one of us would occasionally sob, grieving in that moment for loved ones lost in previous troubles and precarious journeys. My sister Catherine would sometimes tear up while I would try being though like my uncle by holding back my tears. Lewis and Rita were still little, and I don't think they knew much of what was happening other than being terrified. As a Child, I can forget very easily and escape right back into the beauty of the tree canopy.

As we approached the historic Jahkan Valley one of the local travelers gave us a little history of our ancestors in relationship to the valley. It had been a battle ground many years ago for local tribes who fought over land ownership. The heart of the rain forest had a heavy, rich stillness. Little to no wind made it in there. As we ascended, the unbroken green canopy of trees was below us. I could see the trees sway in the air from the forceful wind. From a far distance came waves of movement from the giant tree branches.

I saw some bugs and brightly colored birds. The birds sang in various tones and notes. It is hard to describe the flowery smell, but it was like earth's entire core elements were in perfect balance, which I had never experienced before. At one point, we reached a less dense forest, where some of the sunlight filtered through. I ran ahead of the group to try and step on the head of my own shadow. This was fun, but it did not go over too well with the grownups.

We rested overnight in a town call Yanawelaken. The tribal chief and villagers welcomed us with happiness mixed with mournfulness because of the dead and horrifying journey of the past. The elders stayed up all night talking war stories while we the kids went to bed lulled by the tranquil peacefulness of Mother Nature.

Days later, after our hurting feet felt much better, it was time to embark on the journey to our final destination, the village of Dokorfree. My grandfather had come from Dokorfree and my father and uncle were born there. We were very special in the area. We were considered to be related to the kingship of the tribe because my grandfather and great grandfather were tribal leaders and town chiefs in Dokorfree and Yanawelaken. The people of Yanawelaken prepared a whole cow in celebration of the family's departure and safe arrival to our destination. It was a big feast and departure party. The next morning at eight a.m., we crossed the river on the edge of the village and started our journey.

Some of the kids' feet were still hurting. Their fathers and uncles carried them on their shoulders and backs. But I was running around in the rain playing monkey moves. In some places of the jungle the air was still and heavy with moisture. While in other areas, a perpetual, cloudy fog enveloped and muffled us. I was a little scared in this area, I ran back to the group. Minutes later, we entered a lighter forest. The sun was shining through; we were surrounded by dappled shades of every vibrant green one could possibly imagine.

Rest after rest, town after town, and greeters after greeters, we continued on. I began to wonder when we would ever reach Dokorfree. Agitation and frustration had set by the time we approached this river with the hugest waterfalls I have seen. The sound was loud and thunderous as it splashed down into the basin. My eye popped out with excitement as I silently stood on the bank. The trees and the vegetation lining the banks of this river were amazing. The nature display was a flamboyant expression of life itself. Literally everything around us was alive and exuberant. It looked like everything was breathing, growing right before my naked eye as the forceful air from the water falls blew through. There was a monkey bridge few feet down from the water fall that we used to cross over to the other side. We continued our journey and by sunset, we reached Dokor-free.

Fifteen

A Year of Peace

I WOKE UP THE NEXT morning to the sound of chickens, goats and cows rather than heavy artillery fire. I was gleeful and hopeful again. The bright light from the rising sun made the day seem like war had disappeared from the face of the Earth that moment. Then I heard chattering sound coming from the back of the wooden house. I silently came around to the back to check it out. Uncle Milton and other extended family members were preparing breakfast by the bon fire speaking some strange dialect call Grabo. Surprisingly, they had heard that the war was coming, but had not yet seen experienced blood sprinkling out of the human body after being rattled with bullets or chopped with machetes.

At the back of the kitchen was a wooden fence leading to the backyard. As I walked through that gate, I saw a huge stretch of cocoa farm and children, about five to ten years old, boys and girls, playing among the cocoa trees without clothes or footwear. The palm and coconut trees on this farm were four to six stories tall and full of fruits. There were also oranges, grapefruit, bananas, and plantain, papaya and avocado trees everywhere. This place was a tropical paradise. The floor under this cocoa plantation was clear of vegetation due to the shade from all these plants. With only ten percent of sunlight filtering through, the temperature underneath was mild and cool, good for a hot, sunny day get away. In addition, the wind blowing beneath the canopy made the plantation floor the most graceful and lovely place for a smooth rest and playing games for the little kids in the village.

I got myself settled in my new home. I was the village super star and celebrity coming from the city with some cool shoes and clothing. Kids in the village ran around without clothes or feet wear because their parents could not afford it. Day after day I was presented with food and a live guinea fowl, chicken, goats, or cow. I was incredibly flattered since a cow is quite a generous present and fairly overwhelmed by all the children hanging around, just waiting to see what I would do next. Village life had a slower pace than what I was used to after the tense war zones in other part of Liberia. I would wake up around 5:30 to fetch water for the day's activities and start cooking with other kids in the household.

The men would then go out to the farms for a day of weeding and the women would either head to the farms to weed or start one of their many other chores around the house. Uncle Lister, my father's younger brother who currently lives in Canada, was the strongest farmer in the village. The Giplaye family, in general, was known for their hard work. They grew most of what they ate on a few acres of land. My favorite part of the work was learning how to dry cocoa seed to export it for making chocolate.

On most nights, we played in the moonlight for hours before going to bed. Reading in the moonlight also happened, and I thank God I still have 20/20 vision. Most days brought the thrill of the rainforest and jungle. All farms were made by creeks, rivers or lakes in the middle of the jungle. Many afternoons as we traveled to the farm, we saw different species of animals like monkeys overhead in the canopy eating fruits, seeds and leaves. Some even hung upside down using only nails and feet to hold on to branches. Other land animals followed the monkeys under the canopy eating what the monkeys let fall. Turtles and other small animals crossed our paths all the time. These sightings were fascinating for me as a kid. On the other hand, the locals said sightings like this could also be dangerous because lions and other large predators could use this opportunity to snatch prey.

Sixteen

Near Drowning Experience

ONE TRANQUIL, WARM SUNDAY AFTERNOON, all the kids with some adults, went fishing and swimming at the Butuo River. Nearly everyone caught a fish and this sweet-tasting but bony fish would be served for supper later that evening. My Uncle James and I paddled the dugout canoe up stream to find less disturbed water for fishing for more catch. The village kids swimming down river had driven the fish away.

The water was dappled by shadows cast by tree branches extending over the river. Literally hundreds of water spiders and other bugs skated delicately on the surface. My uncle told me how he had seen an alligator resting in the same spot during sunset weeks earlier. I asked why the children weren't afraid to swim in the same river as these beautiful but dangerous predators.

"For many years, reptiles, amphibians, mammals, ants, spiders and the people of the Grabo kingdom have lived along side each other in peace," my uncle replied. "We continue to live here like our ancestors did centuries ago. We fish, hunt and farm this land to survive and living in harmony with the land and river's power is what makes us who we are today."

About two hours later, we paddled our way back to the other kids downstream. They were still swimming and appeared to be having a blast. Little children exhibited coolness and proficiency about swimming. They were literally flying off the tree branches that cast over the river about forty feet above the water. The happy, little kids yelled, clapped and whistled praises for each person who flew off the tree branch; this inspired my confidence and made me think I could do the same.

I said to myself, "I learned how to swim when I was little in a neighborhood pool in the city. It is about time to teach these country boys and girls some moves. I was wearing my shoes which I did not take off when I jumped off the tree branch, demonstrating my youthful naïveté. I was about to find out that the river was not as shallow as I imagined. But I remember only the following horrifying details.

Grasping the tree branch desperately, I let go and jumped. Tranquil shafts of sunlight wavered in the water below me. I tried to grab onto something for help, but failed to find any sort of handhold. Alone and sinking downward, a shrill series of screams left my young mouth, but my voice vanished in the cold thin air as soon as they were uttered, transformed into mute gabbles. An eternity later, the heavy water darkened around me. My limbs quickly grew weary from frantic leg peddling. My lungs ached. The water around me changed from clear transparent to crystallite bubbles from all the struggling. I was in some deep trouble.

Choking and paddling my hands everywhere in the river, I had horrifying feelings and thoughts about my death: "Oh God, why should I die now, when the rebels did not kill me?"

A hand reached down into the shadowy depths and yanked me upward to the bright light and air. My Uncle

James Komoteh pulled me out of the water and laid me on the river bank. Gasping and shivering, I realized that one of my cool shoes and my underwear had vanished off my body during the struggle. Here I was lying there naked with one shoe on and the other missing, trying to catch my breath.

Seventeen

Journey for Gold and Diamonds

BY THE END OF 1991 and beginning of 1992, I was fed up with the increasing abuse done by rebels in the Dukorfree village. Thirteen-years-old now, I became frustrated that my siblings and I were living in constant fear and abuse of these rebel with no protection from older relatives because everyone was very consume in protecting their own interest. So I decided to travel to the Gold Camp and find some money that would help transport my siblings and me out of the country through the Ivory Coast. I heard some village men were taking some rice to sell in Gold Camp. But the message came very late and I had no rice or food to travel with. Since I had nothing to carry for food, I decided to walk miles into the forest to our old farms and find some plantain, and other fruit that I could travel with without my uncle taking notice. I dug a two-foot hole in the ground and buried the plantain so it could get ripe before the three-day journey to Gold Camp.

But when I came back home, I heard that the village men left two days ahead of schedule because they wanted to trick the witchcraft in the village for a safe journey. So I left my plantain in the forest and decided to follow these men, hoping I could catch up with them as they took a series of rests at rest stops which were mostly on the banks of big rivers. For an entire day, I traveled through the fearful jungle without coming in contact with any humans. There were a couple of small farms and villages along the way where I hoped I could find some people to tell me how long ago the men from Dukorfree village had come through. But all of these small farm villages were empty and abandoned because of the fear that the rebels were coming. I started to cry, because I was terrified that I would be eaten by wild animals or drown in one of the rivers because I did not know how to swim very well. This jungle around Dukorfree was known for its wild predators, most especially big snakes like boas and anacondas and alligators living in these large rivers.

I continue my journey mostly running and jumping over logs lying across the little path. I walked the whole day without seeing any humans following me or coming from the opposite direction. All I could hear were birds singing from tree tops and my heavy breathing and heart beat rising through my chest as I ran. When I got hungry I would find a wild fruit tree and approach with caution making sure there were no monkeys or wild animals under the tree and pluck some really fast as I looked around, watching out for any danger. By nightfall, I heard some human voices coming from a big river right next to a big village called Chilie-Jarpoken. I got some help crossing the river from a stranger who was kind enough to bring his canoe across for me.

He and his wife offered me a place to sleep that night, so I could rest for the two-day journey that lay ahead. I asked if he saw the men that came through. He told me, "Son, you will not catch up with those men because they came by hour ago chanting and singing and moving very fast through the village."

I took off the only pants and shirt that I had and tied a cloth around my waist. After I washed my clothes in the river, I squeezed the water out and hung them over the bon fire to dry for the next day's wear.

The next morning, the family made me some breakfast and his wife packed me some food to travel with. She did not want me to leave. She said, "You are too little to travel that dangerous forest all by yourself." Some villagers were journeying to the next village which was an hour away. So I tagged on with them, hoping to find another group of individuals travelling to the next village. The villagers sang and told stories, mostly fun stories, to make the road trip pleasant. I joined, singing tribal songs and telling old folk tales. But when the villagers reached their final destination and I exited the village all by myself, total silence set in and complete fear took over.

For the next six hours before nightfall, there were no other small villages along the way, just jungle, rivers, valley and mountains. At about twelve in the afternoon, the skies were completely clear and blue, the sun standing in the middle. A breeze began to blow through the forest causing ripe fruits and branches to snap off at a distance in the jungle. The echoes sounded like a squeaking noise that made me pick up my pace and run even faster. The more the wind blew, the more noise resonated from the jungle from broken tree branches, and the more I ran. The clouds rolled over and the blue sky became dark. Heavy rain followed, with thunder roaring and lightening cracking. But I did not stop, I kept going. My clothes became soaked from the rain fall but I kept running as I whipped off the rain water dripping down my face. I did more running that walking all day. On one occasion, I had to hide in the foot of huge tree because tree branches were falling on the road, snapped off by the heavy wind and lightening. By night fall, I made it into the village with the little bag of raw rice mixed with beans the woman in the village had given me. The rice was swollen from the rain fall, and I had to dry it out under the sun the next day before I started my final journey to Gold Camp.

Gold Camp was no place for a thirteen-year-old boy; it definitely was a man's land. The large, inaccessible rainforest and jungle area in the south east lowlands of Liberia was mainly inhabited by the Grabo tribal population which I belong to. Tropical diseases and only an irregular river transport made this region virtually lost. There was a high presence of malaria, and the rebels used this route to traffic marijuana to all parts of the southeast region. The gold found in the jungle rivers and rich land of Liberia was the only hope for many in this area, although most never found what they dreamed about. We made about ten bucks a day compared to the general population living on less a dollar a day.

Man exploited women and children gold-miners while we worked in the tropical climate, mired in the gold and diamond bearing mud, searching for gold and diamond dust. I and my crew did not give up our effort simply because there was no other way to make a living. Our choice was farming, gold and diamond mining or becoming a child soldier. Farming was not paying off as everyone had escaped from the farms to hide from the rebels. So it was a bad harvest season. There was no food; the little food that was available became more expensive. My duties as the youngest child on the twenty-six man crew was fetching water for the women to use to cook and bringing the food to the miners. Some days, when one became sick or died, I had to step in as a replacement until Mama Mary as we called her – the owner of the company – could find a replacement.

One day, I was with four men crew that went on a discovery mission to find a gold mine in a new river discovered in the middle of the jungle. After two days of walking through green rainforest, carrying some raw cassava, plantain and rice, we got to this huge river. When the word spread to towns and villages in the area, that there was gold in the jungle, more than a 2,000 men and women left their homes and families in search of gold. At the height of the gold rush, one liter beer bottle full of yellow gold was carried out daily from the open pit adjacent to the river banks. A multitude of mud-covered bodies crawled up the steep, red-cliffs of the mine like ants rounding up to protect their queen, each person with a sack of earth slung over his or her shoulder. Every ounce of gravel in those sacks contained precious amounts of gold. From a distance, the ground itself seemed to move, as hundreds upon hundreds of men and women climbed up and down wooden ladders made from sticks and ropes taken from the forest. The scene was apocalyptic.

I look back on this time as a rare treat and a remarkable look at what was perhaps the greatest and last gold rush of the Twentieth Century in Liberia. We built halfway tents underneath the floor of the forest using wild palm tree branches for roofing. Heading up river into the darkness, there was no way to tell where the water met the jungle and the only sound was the buzzing noise of the water falls below and above the river. This was the first time any of us ever saw this river, we did not have a name or knew the name for it yet. We built log-bottomed boats from light weight logs and bamboo trees. Every night, we took turns on watch for intruders, rebels, or wild animals.

Two months later, things changed. It was about four a.m., and I was on watch duty with three adults. I heard the low roar of rapid sounds and movement, and someone on the bank signaled to us with a flashlight. I woke up the others, and we jumped into the bamboo boat and steered into a side creek to see who it was. I thought it was new arrivals who had heard about the new gold rush. Their headlamps flashing in the dark, a line of guys with AK-47s jumped into the murky water. Some carrying heavy sacks of rice; I knew instantly this was a rebel take over. With small flashlights clenched in their teeth, the twisting trail of humans from the jungle made their way to the shallow crossing point of the river.

I ran down the river bank pulling on ropes with empty cans attached to them, making a clunking sound that woke everybody up from their sleep. With some people half asleep and others disoriented, everyone came out of their tents shouting the names of God, parents, brothers and sisters. I was able to escape with some team members who had no clue as to what to do because they have not seen a major war before. We all jumped in the boats in the midst of the chaos to cross to the other side of the river. The rebels heard the noise and commotion so they opened fire on us. Shouting in every direction we ran. After some time, they stopped shouting at us, and I thought we were home free. But this was their tactic when they have an ambush set that we were going to fall into. As we approached the middle of the river, the rebels on shore on the other side of the river started shouting at us. My companions panicked and jumped overboard into the river. But I lay flat in the boat because I was afraid I might drown if I jumped. The current of the river took the boat downstream about a mile. After I was out of the line of fire, I lifted my head and pulled on the tree branches lining the river and was luckily able to pull myself ashore.

I turned and looked through the darkness. I could still see my friends, team mates and others screaming, fighting to stay afloat, but drowning in the current of the river. Only a few were able to swim across the river alive. The rebels laughed as the miners struggle to stay afloat. Eventually, their screaming stopped echoing through the forest. I saw their hands move slowly and eventually stop.

Those of us, who survived the attack, ran through the forest to find our way back to town. We made our way through small villages that had been burned to the ground. We kept walking and bypassing some of these destroyed villages. Some were burned so badly, I could see the dark cloud looming against the sky from a distance. We had agreed to walk all night until we made it to Gold Camp safely. During the day, we would search for food and take turns sleeping. At night, it felt as if we were walking with the moon. It followed us under thick clouds and reappeared miles later when the cloud disappeared. It would gradually fade away as the sun rose the next morning.

Two days later we finally arrived at Gold Camp.

Eighteen

Attack on the South-Eastern Region

IT WAS THE BEGINNING OF another peaceful day in the village of Dukorfree, when all young boys and girls left for the farm to work. Some farms were hours away, while some were minutes away from the village. Parents, most especially women, were left at home to cook and bring in food for lunch after a hard morning's work. The afternoon had not come when we heard echoes of gun shots through the deep forest. Moments later, few men made it out of the village alive to the farm and rounded up everyone (women and children). The emotional impact was big. It felt like the world had collapsed around us, and there was no good news from the escaped men as we all stood with our bodies jittery and shaky.

The peace that had prevailed for a year, through 1991 in this part of the country, had ended. Charles Taylor troops attacked in the Southeastern Region in search of government troops which had all escaped before the rebels arrived. This made the rebels angry. They believed that the local villagers were keeping some of the government and Krahn tribal people in hiding. The rebels started torturing and killing people while burning one village after the next down to the ground.

As the rebels captured the villages, they took the women as sex slaves and turned the young men into child soldiers by means of torture. There was no pity for the villages, you either killed or were killed. Killing had become part of our daily routine. Our innocence had been taken away by way of guns and violence without us even realizing it.

My Cousin James joined the rebels because he was tired of being tortured. I was relieved that he had joined because now I had someone who could prevent these guys from beating on me every day. He told me that they were going to raid the next town the next morning.

"Really?" I said.

"Yes, and you can come if you want to, you know."

"No thanks," I said.

Moments later his commander came. "Small soldier!"

"Yes, sir!"

"It is time to go," said the commander.

I ran to the house and told his father about his recruiting, to see if there was any possibility that his dad could talk some sense into him. But that did not work. I came running; they had gathered in the village square singing and dancing in a circle as they fired their weapons into the air. Suddenly, right after that, they were to get in a single line moving down a dusty path to the next village for raiding. Most of the young boys that joined the rebels in the south eastern region did it for revenge.

When Charles Taylor troops and government-sponsored militias systematically attacked villages on the border of the county of Grand Gedeh and Ivory Coast, killing many of the inhabitants, Uncle Milton, Uncle Lister, Catherine, Rita,

Lewis and I lived at the farmhouse for more than six-months. We were with a group that was mostly orphans or separated from extended families. Many of us had avoided capture or death because we were away from the villages harvesting rice and other cash crops on farms thirty to ninety minutes walk from the villages. We were able to flee and hide in one of the dense jungles of Africa, the Liberian rainforest known as the Sarpo National Park.

We hoped that some of the children's parents would come looking. Our food, medicines and clothing come primarily from the farms and the rainforest. After a month, a hunted man from the Krahn tribe showed up on our farm jittery and petrified for his dear life. The smell of fear and fear of death was all over this fellow. Most people in the group said it was too risky to keep him in any group and the best thing would be to let him keep going through the jungle.

He looked emaciated, weak and sickly to me. So I told them that because I knew the forest, I would show him the way. I took him and hid him at the edge of the farm where it bordered the rainforest. Every day I carried this stranger some food that we prepared. He told me stories and taught me how to set wild animal traps and make a trapping basket for shrimps, crabs and lobsters. Weeks went by before my friends realized that I was keeping this man on the farm without their knowledge. I got a severe beating for this before we all escorted him through the Sarpo National Park and left him to find his way home to Grand Gedeh.

Even though we virtually unaffected by the outside world and what was going on in those villages around the jungle for some time, our lives were still in danger. We all cultivated crops, went hunting, gathering, and fishing to supplement our food supply from the farms. The oldest in our group, named Kamoor, heard the rumors from the next farm over that some of the local boys from villages in the area had joined the rebels to push back the government forces and now they were heading our way, to all farms and villages in the rainforest.

We left the national park after that. We traveled by foot for years in search of safe refuge, on a journey that carried us over a thousand miles across three countries to various villages in Maryland County at the southern tip of Liberia where we sought refuge and to refugee camps in Ivory Coast, Guinea, and Ghana.

Over half of us died along this epic journey from starvation, dehydration, sickness and attacks by wild animals and enemy soldiers. During the dark nights in the jungle, my soul grew worried. When it all seemed hopeless, abandonment was rampant within the group and despair waited around the corner. But I did give up hope of surviving those moments.

Sadly, wounds became infected. Littlest ones became too weak or tired to walk, but resting was no option. The older ones in our group carried them on their shoulders. One of my extended cousins named Chea was on this epic journey with his two little sisters who became very weak, he carried one by running and catching up with the group and then ran back to bring the other sister he left at the mercy of wild animals. For us, the Giplaye family, Milton, Catherine, Rita, Lewis and me, this was just the replay of bad dreams.

During this journey, in the deep forest, the strong breeze caused tree branches to snap off posing danger of head injuries. The echo sounded like two eighteen wheelers crashing head-on. We would all be frightened and would stand in silence and listen attentively before moving on. The wild wind picked up its pace. The leaves of the trees began to beat against each other making waves of musical sound that sounded like high pitched electrical drums. After moments of sunshine, came hours of rain. In some deep parts of the forest, we were protected from brutal rainfalls reaching the floor of the jungle. But in some places, the rain came through and wet us down pretty hard. For hours we were all shivering, our fingertips pale and wrinkled.

Than an hour later we would come to an opening in the forest, mostly on mountain tops and Rocky River banks where the sun shined through. We would stop to dry off and probably make a fire to roast some cassava.

During the night, wild cats roared from a distance as the purring of the waterfall echoed for miles through the forest. We took turns adding firewood to the fire during the night as we all slept around it before it completely died out.

During the day, the sunrises and some sunlight filtered through the thick rainforest to reach our path on the forest floor. It became bright from one minute as it surfaced from behind the clouds, and then resurfaced again. We had no watch to tell what it was. But I learned from my uncle that when the sun reached the middle of the sky, it was about 12 noon.

Days before arriving in the Ivory Coast, with no end in sight, some in the group became too exhausted to go on. Some with infected wounds on their bodies went into septic shock and they simply fell to the forest floor or river banks. With no strength to get up, they died. Some families choose to bury their dead, while others just covered their dead with broken tree branches.

Our arrival at refugee camps in the Ivory Coast speaks to the strength of the human spirit to survive and grow under even the most graceless circumstances of twentieth-century civilization.

Nineteen

FROM 1993 TO MARCH OF 1996, I had a relatively peaceful life travelling from one refugee camp in Ivory Coast to the next refugee camp in Ghana. As a sixteen year old boy going on forty, I was not content with living the refugee life. After spending my entire childhood in the shadow of death I would rather die hustling than sitting and standing around in refugee camps waiting for rations to be handed to me. So I decided on a plan to make a good living: a high risk life of transporting government passports for Liberians who wanted to travel abroad but were afraid to go back home and get their passports. Some applied for their passport at the local Liberia Consulate and it took months before they got it, if they were that lucky. I charged $250 U.S per passport. I would collect the required documents, birth certificate, photos and more from each person. To make my trip worthwhile, I had to have at least ten persons. Then I would travel from the Buduburam Refugee camp in Ghana to the refugee camp in Ivory Coast and sneak across the border into Nimba County.

As a teenager, who was young and dumb, I had no idea what I was doing other than living in survival mode all the time. I paid $20.00 U.S. for each passport and an extra

$ 10.00 U.S.to expedite the process to my contact person in the Ministry of Foreign affairs which was then being operated by the Charles Taylor government. He had won the 1997 election that brought some stability in the country. I was left with $220.00 on each passport, giving me a total profit of $2200.00 every trip I made. This was a lot of money for anyone living in Africa when most employed individuals made about $50.00 a month and most households survived on less than a dollar a day, and this was my motivation.

But my luck changed a few days after I arrived in Monrovia on March 26, 1996.

It was a beautiful morning; the cockcrows woke me up from my motel room on the bypass road not too far from the Nigerian embassy. I heard gunshots and heavy fire power erupting in the distance. For a second, I thought it was some kids messing around with leftover fireworks from their New Year's celebration. But when I came out of my room, the street was in disarray as market women hurried with their produce to leave the market. I took the first taxi and went to my friend's house in Congo Town.

That was where I was when the April 6 war began. A new warring faction established by Liberian military men who had escaped to neighboring Sierra Leone had regrouped to attack the Charles Taylor government which they believed to be illegitimate. I had about $800.00 in cash on hand that I would have to use to make it out of Monrovia. But first I had to make it to the Freeport where I had one of the worst memories of the last war.

My friend Eric knew the city very well. Even though he could not leave the country, he was willing to help me get to Freeport safely. We started by making our way down to the Moroccan embassy. As we surfaced out of the bushes, we saw men carrying machine guns, AK-47s, G3s, and RPGs launchers. We dove into the open sewer to hide and found ourselves in the midst of a pile of dead bodies. They still had fresh blood draining from their bodies. One of the bodies I was lying next to had his skull cracked open with his clothes soaked with blood. The lady lying cross section to him was lying on her back with part of her gut protruding out of the cut made by the machetes. Her fingers were still twitching. I felt nauseated and wanted to throw up, but I had to be strong. Making any noise or movement would be deadly for both of us.

The gunshots got louder and louder, so the men got in their Toyota pickup and pulled out. My friend Eric and I got back on the main road and moved toward the city. As we walked there were RPGs flying overhead. My friend Eric and I met a group of strangers who had left their hotels on Old Road and were making their way to the city. A few miles into our journey, the United Nations/ American Red Cross SUV came to help evacuate all foreign nationals. Through a connection of my friend Eric's and by giving them some money, we got them to drop us off around the Doe Community area and we had to make our way back into the Freeport where thousands of people were waiting to board the "Butt Challenge" Ship to Ghana.

Right after we left Doe Community making our way to the Freeport, chattering and laughter came from a distance. We ran and hid in this mud house that had no roof and bullet holes in every inch of it. As we peeked through the hole, I saw men, with no clothes on, carrying sharp machetes and AK-47s, running down this narrow path coming onto the main road in an open square, where the taxi cabs waited for passengers. The naked men were chasing after three men coming towards us. My heart was racing fast and my feet were shaking. They finally caught up with these men and put them in a circle. When I looked, they were chopping them up with their machetes while they cried and begged for their lives. We were hiding in this roofless mud house for at least two hours watching these men mutilate and decapitate the three. Later, they ate some of their body organs while they play soccer with a decapitated head. Later, five men came around the corner, one had no clothes and the others had wigs on. The tall fellow with no clothes on was known as General Butt Naked.

Joshua Milton Blahyi, aka General Butt Naked, cut out the hearts of all three men and took them to be prepared in his soup. I would later came to meet him for the second time under peaceful circumstances on the Buduburam Refugee Camp and listen to him confess and beg for forgiveness from his Liberian victims.

A member of the Sarpo tribe living on the streets of Monrovia, General Butt Naked claimed that at the age of eleven years old, he was initiated as a tribal priest and participated in his first human sacrifice. During the course of the three day ritual that followed, Blahyi says that he had a vision in which he was told by the Devil that he would become a great warrior and that he should continue to practice human sacrifice and cannibalism to increase his power.

According to Blahyi, the Krahn elders appointed him as high priest, to later avenge the late President Doe. Blahyi explained: "I was a high priest for the biggest god under the Krahn tribe, and the late Samuel K. Doe being a fellow tribesman, was automatically placed under my jurisdiction to avenge his death". The Krahn tribe, according to Blahyi, "selected leaders based upon physical prowess through an annual fight. The strongest or last man standing after the bloody contest would take over the birthright and the headship of the tribe".

I sat on the dusty soccer field with group of other victims listening to this young man explain this rubbish. I was so angry, but later realized that the war made most people do a lot of things that they wouldn't have done under normal circumstances. General Butt Naked needed forgiveness from all Liberians most especially from the families whose kids and loved ones he murdered.

He explained that he led his troops into battle naked except for shoes and a gun, hence his nickname. He told us that he believed his nakedness was a source of protection from bullets. Blahyi now claims he regularly sacrificed a victim before battle: "Usually it was a small child, someone whose fresh blood would satisfy the devil." He later explained to an American newspaper, "Sometimes I would enter under the water where children were playing. I would dive under the water, grab one, carry him under and break his neck. Sometimes I'd cause accidents. Sometimes I'd just slaughter them." In January 2008, Milton-Blahyi testified before to Truth and Reconciliation Commission created under current Liberian President Ellen Johnson Sirleaf. He claimed that he killed 20,000 people during the Liberia war.

Blahyi had a religious experience in the refugee camp and became a follower of Jesus Christ. Today, he is President of the End Time Train Evangelistic Ministries Inc., with headquarters in Liberia.

HANS AND SIBLINGS AT REFUGEE SCHOOL IN GHANA

HANS ON REFUGEE BOARDING SCHOOL GHANA

Twenty

Refugee Life

AFTER A MONTHS-LONG, TORTUROUS JOURNEY, we found shelter in a squalid tent in our neighboring country Ivory Coast where French is the primary language. My family and other Liberians refugees were dependent on handouts of food in most cases; the refugees had no clean drinking water or access to health care to prevent outbreaks of cholera, dysentery and hepatitis. Malaria and other insects' transmittable diseases were epidemic. There were dangerous situations around us; this was a different kind of war.

During the escape we sometimes managed to grab a few basics, but most of the time we were just happy to escape with their lives intact. Usually we ended up with thousands of others in a settlement that could stretch for miles. Mothers were still scrambling around looking for their lost children at polling stations, the Red Cross, and United Nation offices. This is a refugee camp, a place not one of us would willingly choose to inhabit even though most people came from poor backgrounds. But it was better than getting slaughtered.

The Ivorian citizens were not nice at all to us. They harassed and intimidated us all the time. We had to travel in groups or risk being beaten by Ivorian gangs or police. However, as refugees we had no choice. Having fled conflicts of unimaginable proportion, massacre, genocide, and other atrocities, we were relieved to have found a safe place. We formulated our thoughts and started constructing tents and other makeshift shelters from whatever materials happened to be available, sticks, plastic sheeting, mud and stones. In the best of cases, humanitarian aid agencies provided the basics: food, clean drinking water, and rudimentary health care. But sometimes, depending on the local political climate and the accessibility to the camp, weeks could go by before help arrived.

That is more than enough time for water-borne diseases such as cholera and dysentery to take hold and spread quickly among thousands of people gathered in these makeshift settlements. Our hope was dried up and our dreams were gone. We were all in total despair, hoping that we would be resettled quickly to a safe place, or, even better, return to the homes we had left behind. After all, a refugee camp was intended as a temporary solution, not a permanent residence. But today, some people still reside in these camps after more than twenty years, sitting around under tents and in the shade of trees, arguing about world politics and making jokes about the war.

We would wait at a location where there was one telephone in a little room, hoping that a relative could call from the United States. We did not have money, so when one person was lucky enough to get a call from relatives, we would all give them the phone numbers of our relatives so they could call our family and let them know that we were waiting for their phone call at this one location.

It was hard to imagine, but some refugees ended up living in these camps for much longer than expected because they failed their resettlement interviews to travel overseas, or could not be resettled in other countries due to restrictive asylum policies. We were literally being warehoused in these refugee camps. As the days went by, the Ivorian government became more restrictive on camps and segregated settlements, and deprived us of our basic rights for years to come. However, some Liberians started to learn how to speak French, and began navigating the local cities like Daninaa, Man, Tabou, San Petro and more to make a living. But my uncle did not like this idea because the Ivorian police was still very brutal to the refugees. So he decided we would leave for Ghana.

In the Buduburam Camp in Ghana, some days we were become hopeful; kids will play in over hundred degree weather for hours on end. Many times we sat at the camp entries with rusty wheelbarrows waiting to push one of the market women's bag of cassava, rice or plum sack into the camp for a little money just to afford an ice water for a day. But then the rainy season set in between the months of May and November. With these heavy rains, came an outbreak of cholera in the camps complicating the situation in the overcrowded refugee camp, where aid efforts were already hampered by insecurity. Devastatingly more people started to die again. Rains and flooding had affected the trucking of water to parts of the camps, and we feared that some refugees would resort to using unsafe water from flooded areas. Before the cholera would be contained, hundreds would be buried.

RITA, LEWIS AND HANS IN BUDUBURAM REFUGEE CAMP 1993

One night as I sat in the gloomy moonlight gripped with fear and sobbing after burying some of my friends who had made it alive from the war zone in a town called Tabou located in a neighboring country call Ivory Coast. The camp was roaring; men and women were crying in every tent around me. By morning, we buried more bodies and more were quarantined. By night fall, a neighbor of mine buried his entire family, wife and five kids. After burying the last son he did not return home. From the graveyard, he crossed the border and returned into the rebels' territory. He would rather be murdered with a gun than the disease that took the life of his entire family.

In this refugee camp in the Ivory Coast, Uncle Milton, Rita, Lewis, Catherine and I were reunited with Aunty Emma, our grandmother, and little brother Matthew that got hurt in the bomb blast. Miraculously, they had been in the Yekepa Hospital receiving care and were evacuated to avoid the next wave of rebel attacks along with some foreign doctors and missionaries who had also been hurt and were being treated at the hospital. During the evacuation, U.N. convoy could not travel through the war zone to make it into Monrovia. So they had to go over the border between Liberia and Ivory Coast which was shorter and less dangerous. The U.N. took the most severely wounded and women with children on the space they had left which is how my family members were lucky to escape the rest of the war.

Before life-saving aid, namely food, water and healthcare could arrived, it was too late for most families. The aid workers finally figured out that to prevent such deaths they would have to educate the population. They increased levels of chlorine distribution, which kills cholera-causing bacteria at water points in the camps. People were trained to monitor and make sure we maintained chlorine use at the correct levels. This really helped.

Meanwhile, they promoted good hygiene practices among the refugees, especially the use of latrines and hand washing with soap. Each refugee received 250 grams of soap with the latest food distribution and this continued monthly for several months. Few months later, vocational learning centers were built by the U.N. and other relief agencies to train and educate refugees on how to make soap, constructions work, art and more. This was good for my uncle and other adults, because it took their minds off the nightmare they endured during the war.

Nonetheless, the major problem looming over these camps was malnutrition among children under five years of age. Refugees at both camps just arriving off the ships had extremely poor physical health and even worse emotional issues, with many families losing children to malnutrition in route or after arrival in the camps before health aid could be provided. A fellow told me about corpses of men, women and children being thrown overboard from the ship to avoid more diseases from spreading. Even on the ship after they left the war zone, it was not safe. A ship called "Butt Challenge" was leaky and the sea was so rough that sea water over flowed onto its decks. To survive this journey, strong and weak had to use buckets to empty the sea water back into the ocean to prevent the ship from sinking. Health and nutrition programs were set up by various experienced partners to address malnutrition, especially among the youngest children, but progress was not fast in coming. More than 1,000 people died from cholera in Ivory Coast refugee camps alone; another 6,000 fell sick during those early days of arrival to the refugee camps and hundreds had died.

Twenty-One

Starting the Healing Process

IN APRIL 1997 DE-TRAUMATIZING workshops were set up to help people face their frightening pasts and even talk about it. I was chosen to be part of the reconciliation committee. Our job at the time was to go door to door and convince refugees to come for the workshop. We told people, the more we talk, and the more relieved we will feel. If Liberia could talk about what happened, it would be the first step towards recovery.

Konneh, who was a eleven years old when he saw his sister brutally killed after being raped multiple times, said that talking with friends like me helped him sort out his memories. Konneh was always the quite one and even more malnourished because he missed his mother badly and was very worried about their where about. But with the help of friends, playing out in the hot sun and doing yard work to afford some food for a day did help us escaped the horrific memories of our past experiences.

Konneh:"We will never forget a single scrap of truth about the civil war," Konneh, added. "We had been running the whole night trying to make our way to the Freeport to catch the ship leaving for Ghana that morning. After my father was killed, they took turns raping Miata, my sister, as a watch hiding in the cabinet underneath the kitchen sink without making a sound. When they were done raping her, they took her away as one of their sex slaves. Since then, I don't know if she is alive or has been killed. My mother was at the red light market when the attack happened. I thought since everyone was running to make ship at the Freeport that morning, my mother would be there too. But that was not the case, the last hour before the ship departed; Prince Johnson attacked the Freeport thinking that some government troop would be on that ship.

"All those trying to find their loved ones before leaving gave up their searches and started fighting for a spot on the ship. I was very lucky. I told one of Ghanaian peacekeepers that my mother was already on the ship. So he wrapped his gun on his shoulder and carried me in his arms to get me on board. After he got me on and told an older man to help me find my mother and he went down into the ship, and I never saw him again. But he really saved my life.

"Many people scrambling to find their way on board the ship in fear for their lives fell over board and drown in the ocean, while others got severely wounded."

Konneh continued to search for his mother like many other children at the camp. Any time there were new arrivals, I and Konneh with other friends would all run to the local UN office to look among the crowd and also check the bulletins. For years, most children kept looking and hoping that someday their parents would be among those new waves of refugees arriving to Buduburam. Instead, they frequently received news of deaths.

We shared our memories. We talked about them in the evenings at meetings at a location called "The Women's Center." As the sun set and the moon light broke over the tents of Buduburam refugee camp, we shared with each other. We were not interested in making things up any more or exaggerating or hiding things. We were no longer muddled by the fear of machetes, but free to let out our feelings and nightmares.

Talking about what happened could be good for other people too. Sometimes another man's or woman's story would help someone else to heal. Comfort Dweh, a young Liberian girl from Pleebo in Maryland County, denied she had been hurt, even though she had large, visible scars on her inner thighs. Not until she heard another girl talking about an attack did she dare to tell anyone about her own horrifying experience and the painful reason why she did not die: they kept her alive to sexually assault her by taking turns.

Comfort Dweh: "I bled, every night, but pretended to love it because I wanted to stay alive.

"When all hope seemed to be lost, I sat in the gloomy cold mud house, waiting for the next armed man to come through the cloth door and rape me over and over. But I prayed for God to grant me favor of life so I could see the daylight of another day and free someday."

Hearing someone else's story helped Comfort realize that the same thing had happened to other people. She was not alone and someone else understood her pain and sorrows.

When you lose your loved one, it's like you made a mistake. You are ashamed. Being a survivor or an orphan or a widow, these weren't things we could have or had accepted easily. Many people just lost interest in life; most especially my Uncle Milton Giplaye who lost his wife and kids in that early bomb blast that took the lives of seven of my family. I encouraged him to attend the meetings, but he refused.

Women who had lost their husbands or their children would say, 'Why have I survived? Am I better than my children?' They would blame themselves for being alive." Some women were even forced to sleep with their own sons, or else both would have been murdered.

Sarah Quah: "After this abomination happened, my son and I were ashamed look at one another in the eyes. We went our separate ways after we left that checkpoint, and that was the last time I ever saw my son alive. Today I wish I had had the courage to have him stay with me through those rough journeys. I do not know if he is alive or dead. I go to sleep every night and pray to see him turn up some day among these new arrivals or to hear from some that he is alive and living in some part of the world."

Decontee, a healing and reconciliation worker who was the lead therapist for the support group said that the de-traumatizing process was like surgery for the mind: "The trauma is so heavy, compared to the emotional strength we have. If it remains inside it can't heal - it needs to be opened.

"But these are not things most people want to talk about. Why should you have to deal with it? People are carrying some horrible issues. Pain destroys your feelings, it destroys your thinking. I personally feel broken and abandoned, I always felt like I was not OK."

I explained to my friends about my stories as we hustled the streets, cleaning gardens and other hard labor. I knew that thinking about what happened would re-open the wounds but that was the best we could do for ourselves. You felt afraid again, horrified again, ashamed, angry, and help-less or confused again. You felt like you'd get lost in it all again. You felt like you might die just by explaining or writing, but this was the only way that I believed we could win this war of atrocities committed against us.

As part of the team that went tent to tent and mud house to mud house inviting people to the Women's Center program every day, I received extra cups of rice and beans from the U.N. food rationing office on the refugee camp. One to two hundred refugees would show up for the meetings, mostly women and their children. Sitting in one big circle, people raised their hands for their turns to pour out their broken spirits and hearts.

While one heart was broken open, others were there to comfort. Tears of hatred were replaced with tears of love and forgiveness. Decontee: "I believe that, despite the pain, realizing that you have been badly hurt and that you, too, need some fixing to be here tonight is an important step towards recovery, hope to see you all next time.

"You have to have sympathy for yourself. It's a long road at head, but it's the start of a new journey to a better future."

Many people will asked, "Once you're aware of how much you've been hurt, what do you do with that? What can you do to stop yourself from being swamped by the horrific memories and the terrible feelings or bad dreams? How can you find a little mental space, a little peace of mind, to let you start picking up the pieces of your life again?"

I noticed that the women carried their babies in one arm and raising their other to ask these smart questions, while most of the men sat around discussing politics and talking revenge for what happened to them and their families.

A strong, tall woman stood up in the back. Shaking and sobbing, she said: "Long before I was born, the traditional justice for murder was revenge. When blood was involved, blood had to be shed from the other family. Revenge was the only option. You kill someone in my family, I kill some-one in yours. 'Eye for an eye.'

"But today, to change our country we must change the past."

When I heard this, I became sad and started to tear up. But deep in my soul, her words were encouraging. Doe, a native man from the Krahn tribe, overthrew President Tolbert, who was an Americo-Liberian. Most native people had been treated as slaves since 1847 by the Americo-Liberians, who were themselves, freed slaves or sons and daughters of freed slaves from the United States of America. Doe murdered most government officials by firing squad which set off the cycle of revenge that had pitted tribe against tribe in the country.

So there was the problem with using revenge as justice: it was a depressing, disheartening, unsatisfactory, destabilizing, demoralizing and toxic way to deal with disputes. Man's inhumanity to man was passed on to the next generation. The cycle of killing continued. No one was happy. Here we all were, lost in a foreign land, bitterly weeping in street corners and dark places for loved ones we had lost. This needed to stop for a better Liberia.

So many questions and so much rage were in the detraumatization meetings. We were sitting on wooden benches in the shade of a large tree when Comfort Dweh told her story of being serially raped. She pointed to Kallon, the person beside her and said, "This is the man who raped me at the checkpoint in Ganta. But I forgave him, and I feel that he's my brother now."

Despite all the talk of forgiveness among Liberian survivors, situations like this were not very common. As Liberians say, recovery is a journey, and people were at different points along that road.

A few would start a fight again tomorrow if they thought they could get away with it; many were just glad to have moments of happiness with friends and family, pleased with the progress that Liberia was making, but still really struggling with the after-effects of the genocide. Through sports like soccer, most adults engaged with the public reconciliation processes, but many found it very difficult. Their stories were stunning. How was that possible? Was it real? If so, what actually happened to make it possible?

Rowland: "I remember the day I decided to join the Rebels. It was after an attack on my village. My parents, and also my grand-father were killed and I was running. I was so scared. I lost everyone; I had nowhere to go and no food to eat. With the Rebels I thought I would be protected, but it was hard. I would see others die in front of me. I was hungry very often, and I was scared. Sometimes they would whip me, sometimes very hard. They used to say that it would make me a better fighter. One day, they whipped my [11-year-old] friend to death because he had not killed the enemy. Also, what I did not like was to hear the girls, our friends, crying because the soldiers had raped them."

Rowland, started sobbing, snuffing while struggling to catch his breath: "I was recruited into an insurgent group (Unimo-K). When I was ten years old, they recruited me in the market place. One of my friends joined up. He was nine. His family was murdered and sisters raped. He said it was very scary in the camp. He held a grenade and had a gun on his shoulder. So I had no choice but to join, and we murdered a lot of people after that. I cannot sleep without having these bad dreams, so please pray for me and help me forget these terrible dreams.

As I listened to my friend, young Tedy-boy, about fourteen years old, I learned for the first time how horrible his story was. We had played soccer during recess from school in the refugee camp like normal African kids, but I came to find out we were all far from normal children because of what we had seen, done to others and endured just to survive the war.

Tedy-boy: "I was working on the farm and heard that soldiers were coming, so my father told me to hide. But I was caught. The soldiers tied me and beat me and took me to a barracks in Bong County. There were many small boys in the warehouse where they brought me. Many of the adults had been by bullets and rockets. They gave me a gun and told me how to use it. I used an AK 47; the adults used RPGs and other bigger weapons. I fired the gun but am not sure if I killed people.

"On the road, enemy soldiers came, and I tried to run away, but a rocket hit the car I was travelling in. Many people were wounded and some others died in the attack. Government soldiers came and took me to Phebe hospital. After a week and two days, an ambulance from JFK hospital came to pick me up. At JFK they amputated my leg. The soldiers gave me a little money while I was in hospital so I paid my way to come to 'Titanic' [a center housing former government militia] from JFK. I was in despair and agony but I did not give up hope. I said to myself, this hell will not be the end of my life. I have to keep going because this may be only the start and the beginning of what God has in store for me. It could have been worse, I lost my parents, my sisters were raped, and I was forced to join the rebels, now I am without a leg. But that is okay because I could have been dead too, but I am here now because God has bigger plans for me."

A soft whispering voice was rising slowly as she cleared her throat in the back. It was Karvina, a fourteen year old girl: "They took us as wives straightaway after they murdered our parents. We had to cook for them while they raped us day after day and night after night. All life stock in our village was slaughtered, and we had to cook it for them. As they came back from the "battle front" as they called it, they would eat and drink, and then they would call for you. They were so many. It was so painful." She sobbed.

"If they went to attack somewhere or to loot, there was always someone who stayed behind. Then he'd call you. If you refused, they used sticks to whip you and sexually abuse you even worse. We mostly stayed in the forest but sometimes we had to go with them and carry what they looted. They all had sex with me. I don't know how many people had sex with me. A man would come, then another and another. I wasn't even the youngest. Some girls were even younger than me. Even the commanders called for you. You couldn't refuse. They said they'd kill you if you ran away. Some people fled and didn't come back. We didn't know if they'd got away or had been killed.

"But every morning I opened my eyes and hoped for a better day. I always hoped and believed we would be saved someday if only we could continue to hold on. Slowly, God answered my cry for help. After months of sexual and physical abuse, a female commander, who was a girlfriend to Charles Taylor, arrived from Lofa and ordered the man to release us immediately. As we crossed behind enemy lines to Monrovia, we got rescued by the American Red Cross."

Lovetee was thirteen when the rebels attacked her village: "We all ran away. But the soldiers captured all the girls, even the very young. You were forced to 'marry' one of the soldiers. If you refused, they would kill you. They would slaughter people like chickens. Wherever we were fighting, along the way, they would take the women and girls working in the fields. They would take young girls, remove their clothes, and then rape them. My 'husband' loved me very much. But one day, he was killed in an attack. I was in danger and decided I should leave. On the way, as I was pregnant, I had my baby. I was alone in the bush, without medication. I still have pain from that painful delivery in the bush. Then I went to the village of my 'husband's' parents, but it was too late, the town was on fire with bleeding corpses lying everywhere. I was afraid those evil men would find me and capture me again, so I ran back into the forest for days living a very primitive life. The Second Liberian Civil War began in 1996 and ended in October 1997 before I came home to my family. "

I have heard Liberians often talk about forgiveness. But I believe forgiveness has become the national pastime. It is an enticing concept, with the potential to break the cycle of slaughtering and avenging like nothing else. But it is not that simple. Like so many of the things Liberia is now doing towards recovery it's incredibly wonderful, it's brave and it's healthy, but for most Liberians it's very, very difficult. I believe we will see this through and Liberia will rise again as one of the prosperous nation in Africa. Liberia will once again be the Lone Star Nation that will shine so bright, that all her children from all over the world will see and come home to for rest and comfort.

Twenty-Two

THE U.N. AND U.S MILITARY intervened to stop the rebel siege on Monrovia in 1996. By the conclusion of that war, more than 250,000 people had been killed and nearly one million displaced. Half that number still had yet to be repatriated in 2005. After considerable progress in negotiations conducted by the United States, United Nations, Organization of African Unity (now the African Union), and the Economic Community of West African States (ECOWAS), disarmament and demobilization of warring factions were hastily carried out and special elections were held on 19 July 1997 with Charles Taylor and his National Patriotic Party emerging victorious. The United States imposed a travel ban on senior Liberian Government officials in 2001 because of the government's support to the Revolutionary United Front (RUF) combatants from Sierra Leone.

COMING TO AMERICA and Life in America

After my journey through hell, an American based organization, Lutheran Christian Services for Refugees, gave my grandmother, Eric, Rita, Catherine, Lewis, Matthew and me a chance to re-unite with our parents and American born siblings in the great United States of America.

Coming to the U.S. with its promise of a better life was a significant and dramatic life changing experience. The Lutheran Christian Services helped us find my father in America and he anxiously filed petitions for me, my siblings and grandmother to come live in the United States. During the interview we did not say much, but showed the amputated heel of my grandmother that happened when the rocket landed on our house in Yekepa. The rest of the family took off our clothes and showed our scars from injuries sustained from metal pieces that came from the grenade's explosion. Luckily, we were given visas to be resettled with our parents in New York City. Uncle Milton was denied a visa until they could prove the relationship between him and my father, his elder brother.

I possessed limited education and English skills. But John F. Kennedy once said, "Our problems are man-made, therefore they may be solved by man. No problem of human destiny is beyond human beings." This would prove to be very true.

Catherine, Rita, Lewis, Eric and I arrived into the United States of America on February 9, 1999. The process of coming to America had started six months earlier with multiple interviews in the refugee camps. The most exciting part of coming to America from the refugee camps was, everyone envied you and wanted to be your friend. It was believed that all your problems in the world would be over once you entered America and you were just a step away from heaven. They wanted to be your friend because they believed you would help them out of their poverty once you entered America because they assumed that money grew on trees in America.

Many friends escorted me to the airport. My family was travelling with a group of about 200 other refugees who were granted refugee status to resettle in America. We boarded the airplane at Abidjan International Airport in the

Ivory Coast. I had never imagined airplanes to be as enormous and gigantic; I always thought they were perhaps the same size as they were in the night sky. This departure day, was like a dream, I could not believed it was finally happening.

Everything about February 9, 1999 was promising. I remember the sun was bright and the sky was blue as the deepest ocean. We were surrounded by a multitude of people, friends and family; some fighting to have their chance of taking a picture with you like a local celebrity in town, some were sobbing while others stood by and watched sadly hoping their day would finally come too.

We boarded Air France to Paris. On the flight, we got served dinner and breakfast. My favorite was the dessert for dinner. Ice cream came in a pure white, plastic cup. I just peeled off the cover. My first taste melted so quickly that I had no time to chew on it. I have kept the ice cream cup.

By morning, we arrived in Paris and two hours later, we boarded United Airlines to America. On an eight-hour flight, we got served fancy food four times, literally every two hours. At this point I knew I was on my way to America. I took a sip of my water with a slice of lemon and then inhaled deeply. The most wonderful, yet familiar, aroma filled my nostrils. I couldn't place it but it smelt like nothing I had tasted before. I kept taking deep breaths and turning my head to see where this delicious aroma was coming from. Sure enough there was my platter of food put in front of me by the air waitress, and it was mine to devour. I said to her, "I don't have any money to pay for all of this."

She smiled pleasantly with her beautiful white teeth shining through her lips and said nicely, "That is okay, just eat."

The wonderful sounding waitress laid down the food and reminded me to leave some room for dessert. Right then dessert was the last thing on my mind, all I wanted was just to eat. I put the fist baked chicken in my mouth. Wow, it tasted GREAT, and the seasonings were just great too.

We arrived in New York at John F. Kennedy airport at 8:00 a.m., twenty hours after boarding the plane in West Africa. The skyline of New York was majestic from the sky. The buildings were so astonishingly tall and eye-catching, I felt like I had traveled in time to another planet. These buildings had the most distinctive architecture I had ever seen in my lifetime. There were so many of them, I could not believe that man was capable of putting them up. The buildings looked like they had plunged from the heaven and landed on earth.

Our parents anxiously waiting outside the immigration gate to welcome us after almost nineteen years; this reunion was emotional. My mother was so excited that she thought she was dreaming. All she did was touch and feel one person at a time to make sure we were real and not ghosts she was seeing. It was a moment to behold and remember, a moment I had prayed for, dreamt about.

Within a week, we encountered the true reality that America offered to its immigrants. My parents had taken a loan to afford the plane tickets for the family to come to America. We stepped on the soil of this nation with practically nothing. I had to find a job to help pay for the plane tickets. We all spoke English with an accent and we were overwhelmed adjusting to the American culture.

On my first outing in New York City from Long Island to the immigration office downtown, I found out that this was definitely just too busy a city for me. No matter where I went, I saw confusion that never seemed to end. There were an endless amount of cars flowing through the streets and honking their horns loud enough to drive me crazy. Some of the vehicles were large rattling trucks that added to the never-ending noise generated by rest of the things around me including the subway system that rattled the earth underneath my feet. I waited my turn to cross a very busy crosswalk without getting hit by a car. Everyone seemed to be in a hurry, having no time to say hi or make eye contact to answer a question if I had one. Smelling of cologne, people passed hurriedly by to make their next bus, train; flight or ferry on time before the sun disappeared below the horizon of the Hudson River and the darkness enveloped the sky to set the stage for the magnificent galaxy of the sky line from the night lights of the city called "The Big Apple."

Down below the surface in Manhattan, the train and subway system was a whole new world in itself. Over my head was the huge departure board with names of stations and corresponding train numbers and departure times. Around me, a mass of people hurried in and out like a gigantic moving snake. Some carried hand bags; others carried their kids while others just carried the walkman listening to music nodding their heads back and forth. Some were dragging rolling backpacks. Some stood and watched attentively for the next train and seemed to be unconscious of anything else going on around them, but they somehow managed not to run into anyone else as they moved swiftly to board the train, almost operating like a time set robotic system. As soon as I went up stairs to ground level, I couldn't help but notice the stench of the city. It was a mix between carbon monoxide from cars, trash, and other indistinguishable things.

As I emerged for underground, onto the streets, I see an endless flow of cars in traffic, many of which are yellow in color and have a small illuminated sign with the word "TAXI" on top. Most of the drivers seemed to dress in long gowns and looked foreign.

When I stepped on the soil of this great nation eleven years ago, I was eager to take advantage of the enormous possibilities that it had to offer especially when it came to education.

Life was hard in the refugee camps; it was not easy for dignified and self-sufficient individuals to be dependent on humanitarian aid, trapped in refugee-hood.

When I arrived at the camp in Buduburam, I was very determined to get an education and I prepared myself to succeed in a U.N. supported accelerated education program designed to fast-track new arrivals into the mainstream classrooms of the Ghanaian school system. I took many tutorial afternoon classes to improve my math, science and English skills, and this paid off. All I wanted to do was to study and become a doctor or nurse someday. The accelerated education program was very important for me. It helped me overcome the seven-year gap of no schooling.

At the time, U.N. had a double promotion system in the accelerated program in the refugee schools. In this system, a smart student who worked hard could be promoted twice in a school year if he or she passed out of courses in higher grades. I got double promoted from the fourth grade to the sixth grade in 1992. By 1994, I was in the ninth grade. Moreover, during all these years and all these classes, I was no less than a class president. By 1998, I graduated from Rainbow Covenant High School with honors and as the student council president.

All this was not easy, it was hard work. Some days, we were forced to learn outside in the heat and dust most especially during examination weeks in order to prevent students from cheating in crowded classrooms. The U.N. erected tents to cope with the increasing enrollment and provided books and basic education materials to help us learn. But it was not enough. Most semesters, I had to use one copybook and one pencil for sixteen subjects. I guarded this one copybook and pencil with my life.

After hearing about Suffolk County Community college from current students in Long Island New York, I was impressed by the diversity, student-faculty ratio, and the social life. I started school with the intension to practice medicine. Being raised in a third-world nation deprived of technology, I realized that I would have to take a technology class in other to benefit and make it through my studies. I also noticed that technology was already an immense part of our daily lives in the United States, and it was expanding every moment. Citizens of developed nations take it for granted, but a refugee like me from jungles to tents on the refugee camps to in third-world nations where life with little to no technology, this meant a lot to me.

I moved to Boston and completed my nursing studies and applied science at the Middlesex Community College and later relocated to Michigan and completed my Bachelor of Science in nursing to give me the expertise and experience that I will need to accomplish my life's aspirations which is helping the sick. To accomplish my profound aspirations to help improve the lives of impoverished people in third-world nations by studying healthcare, I needed not only knowledge, but also experience. I knew it would be hugely beneficial for Africa if I could directly explore the impact of lack of reliable health care services to the poor.

Since my graduation from nursing school in May of 2002, I have worked as a registered nurse (RN) across America in some of the best hospitals in the nation providing service to the sick and needy population. I have also founded a not for profit organization call Acare Human Services. I travel to Africa yearly to help join the fight against malaria, HIV/AIDS and also assist in the improving of health education in schools and villages.

Today, my grandma is now in a nursing home in the state of Delaware. My older sister, Catherine, lives nearby with our parents. Lewis is doing very well as a security officer in Newark, New Jersey. Rita is happily living in Lowell, Massachusetts with her two daughters and working as a certified nurse aide. Unfortunately, Eric who was the child soldier, got deported back to Africa because he was having some trouble with the law.

Sadly, Uncle Milton did not follow the family to America. The process of ascertaining his relationship to my father went on for years. Finally in 2003, all investigations by U.S immigration were clear and he was given a visa to be resettled in the United States of America. A few weeks before his travel date, he went to sleep one night and never woke up the next morning. According to the autopsy, he died from a massive stroke.

His body was transported from the refugee Camp in Ghana to Liberia for a proper burial. This was sudden loss was very scary and disorienting for the family. I personally was very sad and suddenly found myself into an unfamiliar territory that was frightening and unsettling, knowing that I would not see Uncle Milton again after all the hell we went through. I later realized that death is no respecter of persons or time and situation in life. Your time is your time. One can be rich or poor, beautiful or ugly, young or old, educated or uneducated your appointed time of death is your appoint time. This my ideology of life and death that it does not discriminate for age, race, sex, education, economic status, religion, culture or nationality and so on, helped me through my grieving process one day at the time .

I am married with two boys, Hanstin and Akais, and currently living in Grand Rapids Michigan, still working as a registered nurse. I believed life is a journey with many interstates, hills, valleys and crossroads that changes with time, seasons and weather conditions that we must learn to live with. This is the first thirty-two years of my life journey.

GRADUATION FROM Nursing COLLEGE 2002 IN Lowell, MA

"In the End, we will remember not the words of our enemies, but the silence of our friends." Martin Luther King Jr. Today, Liberia's current president, Ellen Johnson Sirleaf, who initially was a strong supporter of war and Charles Taylor, was inaugurated in January 2006 and the National Transitional Government of Liberia terminated its power. After fourteen years of war, Liberians may be ready for development of basic services on peaceful terms, particularly education, access to clean drinking water, basic health needs, electric city and primary infrastructure.

THE END

GEOGRAPHY

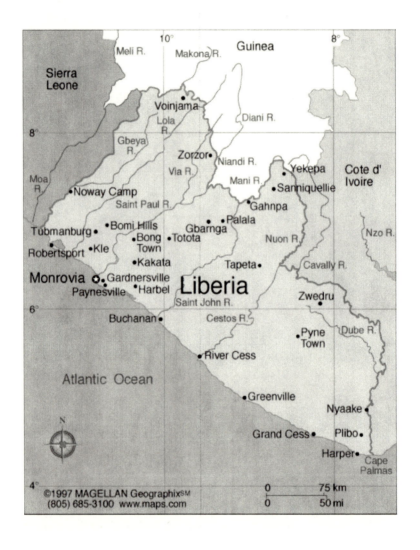

Area: 111,369 sq. km. (43,000 sq. mi.). Slightly larger than Ohio.

Cities: *Capital*—Monrovia (pop. 1,010,970). *Principal towns*—Ganta (pop. 41,000), Buchanan (pop. 34,000), Gbarnga (pop. 34,000), Kakata (pop. 33,000), Voinjama (pop. 26,000).

Terrain: *Three areas*—Mangrove swamps and beaches along the coast, wooded hills and semi deciduous shrub lands along the immediate interior, and dense tropical forests and plateaus in the interior. Liberia has 40% of West Africa's rain forest.

People

Nationality: *Noun and adjective*—Liberian(s).

Population (2012): 3.887 million.

Annual population growth rate (2011): 2.6%.

Ethnic groups: Kpelle 20%, Bassa 14%, Gio 8%, Kru 6%, 52% spread over 12 other ethnic groups.

Religions: Christian 85%, Muslim 12%, other 1.5%, no religion 1.5%.

Languages: English is the official language. There are 16 indigenous languages.

Education: *Literacy* (2008)—58%.

Health: *Life expectancy* (2011)—57 years.

Work force: *Agriculture*—70%; *industry*—15%; *services*—2%. Employment in the formal sector is estimated at 15%.

Government

Type: Republic.

Independence: July 26, 1847 (from American Colonization Society).

Constitution: January 6, 1986.

Branches: *Executive*—president. *Legislative*—bicameral. *Judicial*—Supreme Court, courts of first instance, courts of record, justices of the peace.

Economy

GDP (2011): $1.2 billion.

Real GDP growth rate (2011): 6.9%.

Real per capita GDP (2010): $500.

Average annual inflation (2011): 10%.

Natural resources: Iron ore, rubber, timber, diamonds, gold, tin, possible offshore deposits of crude oil.

Agricultural Products: coffee, cocoa, sugarcane, rice, cassava, palm oil, bananas, plantains, citrus, pineapple, sweet potatoes, corn, and vegetables.

Industry: Agricultural production (61% of 2009 GDP), rubber, diamonds, gold, iron ore, forestry, beverages, construction.

Trade (2010): *Exports*—$207 million (rubber 61%). *Major markets*—India (26.5%); United States (17.9%); Poland (13.9%). *Imports*—$551 million (rice 29%; machinery/transport equipment 23%). *Major suppliers*—South Korea (27.2%); Singapore (25.5%); Japan (11.8%).

PEOPLE

There are 16 ethnic groups that make up Liberia's indigenous population. The Kpelle in central and western Liberia is the largest ethnic group. Americo-Liberians who are descendants of freed slaves that arrived in Liberia after 1820 make up less than 5% of the population.

There also are sizable numbers of Lebanese, Indians, and

other West African nationals who comprise part of Liberia's business community. The Liberian constitution restricts citizenship to only people of Negro descent, and land ownership is restricted to citizens.

HISTORY

Portuguese explorers established contacts with Liberia as early as 1461 and named the area Grain Coast because of the abundance of "grains of paradise" (Malegueta pepper seeds). In 1663, the British installed trading posts on the Grain Coast, but the Dutch destroyed these posts a year later. There were no further reports of European settlements along the Grain Coast until the arrival of freed slaves in the early 1800s.

Liberia, "land of the free," was founded by free African-Americans and freed slaves from the United States in 1820. An initial group of 86 immigrants, who came to be called Americo-Liberians, established a settlement in Christopolis (now Monrovia, named after U.S. President James Monroe) on February 6, 1820.

Thousands of freed American slaves and free African-Americans arrived during the following years, leading to the formation of more settlements and culminating in a declaration of independence of the Republic of Liberia on July 26, 1847. The drive to resettle freed slaves in Africa was promoted by the American Colonization Society (ACS), an organization of white clergymen, abolitionists, and slave owners founded in 1816 by Robert Finley, a Presbyterian minister. Between 1821 and 1867, the ACS resettled some 10,000 African-Americans and several thousand Africans from interdicted slave ships; it governed the Commonwealth of Liberia until independence in 1847.

In Liberia's early years, the Americo-Liberian settlers periodically encountered stiff and sometimes violent opposition from indigenous Africans, who were excluded from citizenship in the new Republic until 1904. At the same time, British and French colonial expansionists encroached upon Liberia, taking over much of its territory. Politically, the country was a one-party state ruled by the True Whig Party (TWP). Joseph Jenkins Roberts, who was born and raised in America, was Liberia's first President. The style of government and constitution was fashioned on that of the United States, and the Americo-Liberian elite monopolized political power and restricted the voting rights of the indigenous population. The True Whig Party dominated all sectors of Liberia from independence in 1847 until April 12, 1980, when indigenous Liberian Master Sergeant Samuel K. Doe (from the Krahn ethnic group) seized power in a coup d'état. Doe's forces executed President William R. Tolbert and several officials of his government, mostly of Americo-Liberian descent. One hundred and thirty-three years of Americo-Liberian political domination ended with the formation of the People's Redemption Council (PRC).

Over time, the Doe government began promoting members of Doe's Krahn ethnic group, who soon dominated political and military life in Liberia. This raised ethnic tensions and caused frequent hostilities between the politically and militarily dominant Krahns and other ethnic groups in the country. After the October 1985 elections, characterized by widespread fraud, Doe solidified his control. The period after the elections saw increased human rights abuses, corruption, and ethnic tensions. The standard of living further deteriorated. On November 12, 1985, former Army Commanding Gen. Thomas Quiwonkpa almost succeeded in toppling Doe's government. The Armed Forces of Liberia repelled Quiwonkpa's attack and executed him in Monrovia. Doe's Krahn-dominated forces carried out reprisals against Mano and Gio civilians suspected of supporting Quiwonkpa. Despite Doe's poor human rights record and questionable democratic credentials, he retained close relations with Washington. A staunch U.S. ally, Doe met twice with President Ronald Reagan and enjoyed considerable U.S. financial support.

On December 24, 1989, a small band of rebels led by Doe's former procurement chief, Charles Taylor, invaded Liberia from Ivory Coast. Taylor and his National Patriotic Front rebels rapidly gained the support of many Liberians and reached the outskirts of Monrovia within six months. From 1989 to 1996 one of Africa's bloodiest civil wars ensued, claiming the lives of more than 200,000 Liberians and displacing a million others into refugee camps in neighboring countries. The Economic Community of West African States (ECOWAS) intervened in 1990 and succeeded in preventing Charles Taylor from capturing Monrovia. Prince Johnson—formerly a member of Taylor's National Patriotic Front of Liberia (NPFL)—formed the break-away Independent National Patriotic Front of Liberia (INPFL). Johnson's forces captured and killed Doe on September 9, 1990. Taking refuge in Sierra Leone and other neighboring countries, former AFL soldiers founded the new insurgent United Liberation Movement of Liberia for Democracy (ULIMO), fighting back Taylor's NPFL.

An Interim Government of National Unity (IGNU) was formed in Gambia under the auspices of ECOWAS in October 1990, headed by Dr. Amos C. Sawyer. Taylor (along with other Liberian factions) refused to work with the interim government and continued fighting. After more than a dozen peace accords and declining military power, Taylor finally agreed to the formation of a five-man transitional government. A hasty disarmament and demobilization of warring factions was followed by special elections on July 19, 1997. Charles Taylor and his National Patriotic Party emerged victorious. Taylor won the election by a large majority, primarily because Liberians feared a return to war if Taylor lost.

For the next six years, the Taylor government did not improve the lives of Liberians. Unemployment and illiteracy stood above 75%, and little investment was made in the country's infrastructure to remedy the ravages of war. Pipe-borne water and electricity were generally unavailable to most of the population, especially outside Monrovia, and schools, hospitals, roads, and infrastructure remained derelict. Rather than work to improve the lives of Liberians, Taylor supported the Revolutionary United Front in Sierra Leone. Taylor's misrule led to the resumption of armed rebellion from among Taylor's former adversaries. By 2003, armed groups called "Liberians United for Reconciliation and Democracy" (LURD) and "Movement for Democracy in Liberia" (MODEL), largely representing elements of the former ULIMO-K and ULIMO-J factions that fought Taylor during Liberia's previous civil war (1989-1996), were challenging Taylor and his increasingly fragmented supporters on the outskirts of Monrovia.

On June 4, 2003 in Accra, Ghana, ECOWAS facilitated peace talks among the Government of Liberia, civil society, and the LURD and MODEL rebel groups. On the same day, the Chief Prosecutor of the Special Court for Sierra Leone issued a press statement announcing the opening of a sealed March 7, 2003 indictment of Liberian President Charles Taylor for "bearing the greatest responsibility" for atrocities in Sierra Leone since November 1996. In July 2003 the Government of Liberia, LURD, and MODEL signed a cease-fire that all sides failed to respect; bitter fighting reached downtown Monrovia in July and August 2003, creating a massive humanitarian disaster.

On August 11, 2003, under intense U.S. and international pressure, President Taylor resigned office and departed into exile in Nigeria. This move paved the way for the deployment by ECOWAS of what became a 3,600-strong peace-keeping mission in Liberia (ECOMIL). On August 18, leaders from the Liberian Government, the rebels, political parties, and civil society signed a comprehensive peace agreement that laid the framework for constructing a 2-

year National Transitional Government of Liberia (NTGL), headed by businessman Charles Gyude Bryant. The U.N. took over security in Liberia in October 2003, subsuming ECOMIL into the United Nations Mission in Liberia (UNMIL), a force that at one point numbered more than 12,000 troops and 1,148 police officers.

The October 11, 2005 presidential and legislative elections and the subsequent November 8, 2005 presidential run-off were the most free, fair, and peaceful elections in Liberia's history. Ellen Johnson Sirleaf defeated international soccer star George Weah 59.4% to 40.6% to become Africa's first democratically elected female president. She was inaugurated in January 2006. The president's Unity Party did not win control of the legislature, in which 9 of the 20 registered political parties were represented.

The political situation remained stable after the 2005 elections. President Johnson Sirleaf has enjoyed good relations with international organizations and donor governments, with whom she has worked closely on Liberia's development. A Truth and Reconciliation Commission (TRC) was established in 2005 to investigate and report on gross human rights violations that occurred in Liberia between January 1979 and October 2003. The TRC's final, edited report was released in late 2009. The Liberian Government has yet to address many of the recommendations.

The Johnson Sirleaf government won substantial donor support for its new poverty reduction strategy at the June 2008 Liberia Poverty Reduction Forum in Berlin, Germany. In order to maintain stability through the post-conflict period, Liberia's security sector reform efforts have led to the disarmament of more than 100,000 ex-combatants, the wholesale U.S.-led reconstruction of the Armed Forces of Liberia, and a U.N.-led effort to overhaul the Liberian National Police. The mandate of UNMIL was extended in September 2011 to September 2012. Within UNMIL's mandate is a Peace building Commission focusing on promoting rule of law, security sector reform, and national reconciliation. However, the Government of Liberia has continued to avoid taking action on freezing assets of former President Charles Taylor and his supporters, as mandated by the U.N. Security Council.